Analysis and Comments on Selected English Cases

Volume I

英国法精选案例评析

第一册

Bilingual

中英双语

Yuxuan Wan

万宇轩　著

法律出版社 | LAW PRESS

北京

图书在版编目(CIP)数据

英国法精选案例评析. 第一册,汉、英 / 万宇轩著. -- 北京 : 法律出版社, 2023

ISBN 978-7-5197-8601-4

Ⅰ. ①英… Ⅱ. ①万… Ⅲ. ①法律-案例-英国-汉、英 Ⅳ. ①D956.1

中国国家版本馆 CIP 数据核字(2023)第 238913 号

英国法精选案例评析(第一册) **YINGGUOFA JINGXUAN ANLI** **PINGXI (DI YI CE)**	万宇轩 著	策划编辑 沈小英 责任编辑 刘晓萌 鲁 安 装帧设计 鲍龙卉

出版发行 法律出版社
编辑统筹 法治与经济出版分社
责任校对 王 丰
责任印制 吕亚莉
经　　销 新华书店

开本 A5
印张 9　**字数** 217 千
版本 2023 年 12 月第 1 版
印次 2023 年 12 月第 1 次印刷
印刷 北京虎彩文化传播有限公司

地址:北京市丰台区莲花池西里 7 号(100073)
网址:www.lawpress.com.cn
投稿邮箱:info@lawpress.com.cn
举报盗版邮箱:jbwq@lawpress.com.cn

销售电话:010-83938349
客服电话:010-83938350
咨询电话:010-63939796

书号:ISBN 978-7-5197-8601-4　**定价**:96.00 元

凡购买本社图书,如有印装错误,我社负责退换。电话:010-83938349

To my beloved mother

谨以此书献给我的母亲

序

中国目前的法学教育评价，使很多人特别是年轻学者更愿意出学术专著，而少有意愿编写教材之类的书籍。缘由很简单，教材之类的成果，对于编写者来说在晋升、考核等中基本得不到或甚少得到评价，且现在编写教材的难度比撰写学术专著的难度大，可谓“吃力不讨好”。我自己编写过国家规划教材，也参与编写过教育部马工程重点教材，很多是“十年磨一剑”，可见要编好一本教材的不易。

前段时间，北京隆安律师事务所的高级合伙人万迎军律师通过法律出版社联系我，告诉我一个好消息，其儿子万宇轩撰写的《英国法精选案例评析》（第一册）即将问世，同时嘱我看看能否为该书写篇介绍。当看到作者的背景，以及书稿清样和主要章节后，我欣然同意。现在摆在读者面前的这本案例精选不是某位法学院著名教授撰写，而是出自一位年仅 21 岁的本科生之手，可谓勇气可嘉，后生可畏，让我着实有先睹为快的感觉。

本书的作者万宇轩，中学就读于著名的北京乐成国际学校，英文优异，获多项荣誉。喜欢绘画和弹钢琴，酷爱足球，曾担任学校 U14 足球队主教练，目前在具有 572 年历史的英国格拉斯哥大学法学院攻读普通法本科专业。万宇轩系统学习了英国法和欧盟法等课程，包括普通法制度、英国宪法、英国合同法、侵权法、英格兰和威尔士刑法、土地法、衡平法和信托法、劳动法、法律和政府、罗马法（财产和义务）、反歧视法、知识产权法、公共国际法、网络犯罪法、证据基础、商业组织、法律体系、欧盟法、英国文学等，还撰写了论文《英国脱欧对英国普通法和成文法的影响》。

作者在完成大学三年级学业后，了解到我国关于英国法的介绍和学习资料比较少，尤其缺乏对英国法案例进行全面研究的资料和书籍。同时，国家实行高水平对外开放和高质量发展政策，对涉外法治人才的培养越来越重视，外国法、比较法等法律教育的需求越来越多，水准要求进一步提高。于是，他就萌生以英文形式原汁原味介绍英国法著名案例并评析英国法官审判思路的想法。其后开始以英国 5 个法律领域（公司法、知识产权法、反歧视法、劳动法、信托法和衡平法）为基础，就每一领域精选 3 个经典案例，通过摘取法官在特定案件中的精彩论断，分析每一级法院法官的审判思路和适用法律的标准，包括对其后案件的影响，如所罗门诉所罗门有限责任公司案以及优步司机诉优步公司案等。前述内容中，英国反歧视法律和案例的介绍尤为独特。

本书是中国人用全英文书写，介绍、分析和评点英国部分法律和著名案例以及英国法官审判思路，其后再由作者翻译为中文，以中英双语出版发行。这种撰写方式乃国内首创，对于法学教材的编写进行了有益探索，具有鲜明的独特性。对于各大法学院的学生（尤其是有志于从事涉外法治工作的学生）和青年律师学习法律英语特别是希望了解英国普通法、衡平法及其判例，具有非常直接的帮助。此外，对于中国法官而言，通过阅读本书而了解英国法官对于公司法、知识产权法等领域特定案件的裁判思路，在外国法的规范形成和具体适用方面，相信也会有所裨益。

鉴于本书是针对实际案例的判决而作出的介绍、分析和评价，自然涉及每一案件的简要具体案情，结合领会法官的分析思路，因此，阅读起来并不枯燥。作者对个别案例的描述采用了场景描述和悬疑描写的方式，读来饶有趣味。

这是作者独立撰写完成的首部就精选英国法案例予以评析的书籍，故定名为第一册。据悉，作者正在选择和确定英国其他法律和相关案例，准备撰写第二册英国法精选案例评析。我与读者一样，期待作者后续案例评析的问世，不断充实我国法学教育中的外国法知识。

非常有意思和巧合的是，作者所在的格拉斯哥大学的守护神之一是独角兽，象征着纯洁；本书出版单位法律出版社的标志獬豸，是中国古代神话传说中的一种神兽，也是独角兽，象征着正义。希望本书能够给读者带来纯洁和正义的启示。

是为推荐。

中国法学会法学教育研究会秘书长
中国人民大学法学院教授、博士研究生导师

CONTENTS

目　　录

CASES

案　　例

Part One: Selected Cases under Company Law

第一部分：公司法案例

案例 1　所罗门诉所罗门有限责任公司案

[1897] AC 22

案例 2　亚当斯诉开普公司案

[1990] Ch 433 (CA)

案例 3　普雷斯特诉派绰德资源有限公司案

[2013] 2 AC 415

Case 1 Salomon v A Salomon Co Ltd
—The rule of separate legal personality

Preface:

The Separate Legal person principle (SLP) in company law is widely known across the globe albeit the differences in the legal jurisdictions , it recognizes that a company is a separate legal person, apart from its shareholders, which has the capacity to both:

1. Enjoy or acquire enforceable legal rights or property; and

2. Be, or become subject to enforceable legal obligations and liabilities.

While this principle is well-established to the population who are familiar with the constitution of companies , how such rule was clarified in early case laws may not be as renowned. In common law and especially the United Kingdom, the case of Salomon v A Salomon Co Ltd [1897] AC 22 and its position on the separate legal person principle influenced the decision of many cases and jurisdictions which followed.

案例 1　所罗门诉所罗门有限责任公司案
——独立法律人格规则

引言：

公司法中的独立法人原则（SLP）在全球广为人知，虽然各个法域存在差异，但是均认可公司是一个独立的法人，与其股东分开，并具有以下两种能力：

1. 享有或获取可执行的法律权利或财产；
2. 作为或成为可执行的法律义务和责任的主体。

虽然熟悉公司组织结构的人群对这一原则足够了解，但早期案例法对该规则的澄清可能并不为人所知。在普通法中，特别是在英国，所罗门诉所罗门有限责任公司（[1897] AC 22）一案及其对独立法人原则的立场影响了随后许多法域和案件的判决。

Facts

Mr Salomon was a sole trader who owned a profitable manufacturing business. As an attempt to run his business as a limited company, he registered a new company he later used to buy his old manufacturing business.

Under the statutes governing company registrations at the time, seven persons subscribed to the memorandum of association: Mr Salomon himself, his wife and five adult children. The purchase of the business, instead of the market value, was priced in "the sanguine expectations of a fond owner" and was ultimately 39.000 pounds. 10,000 out of the 39,000 were paid as a debenture to Mr Salomon which meant it owed such amounts to Mr Salomon, secured by a charge.

Unfortunately and immediately after the transfer, the company found itself in danger of liquidation and unable to pay its debts. After its assets were realized in cash to pay the creditors, it was discovered that not even its secured creditors were able to be paid in full, meaning that Mr Salomon's right of recovery against the loan notes were prioritized over the claims of unsecured creditors, leaving them without any relief. As a result, the liquidator brought an action against Mr Salomon, alleging that the loan notes were fraudulent and therefore invalid, that the company was acting as mere agent of Mr Salomon and the entire purchase was a sham. If the liquidator's claims were favoured, Mr Salomon would be personally liable for the debts incurred by the company just as he

案件事实

所罗门先生是一位拥有一家盈利的制造业务的个体经营者。为了试图将其业务转变为有限公司运营，他注册了一家新公司并在其后用这家新公司购买了其原有制造业务。

根据当时的公司注册法规，有 7 人签订了公司章程：所罗门先生本人、其妻子以及 5 个成年子女。他购买自己先前业务的价格并非市场价值，而是以“充满期待的所有者的乐观预期”为价格，最终定价为 39，000 英镑。其中的 10，000 英镑以债券的形式支付给所罗门先生，这意味着该公司欠付所罗门先生该等金额，并设定了一项抵押权作为保证。

不幸的是，转让完成伊始，该公司旋即面临清算危机且无法偿还债务。在其资产被变现以支付债权人后，人们发现甚至连有保证的债权人也无法得到全额偿还，这是因为所罗门先生对贷款票据的追索权优先于无担保债权人的索赔，所以他人无法得到任何救济。因此，清算人对所罗门先生提起诉讼，声称贷款票据存有欺诈性且因此无效，该公司只是所罗门先生的代理人，整个购买过程是一个骗局。如果清算人的主张获得支持，那么所罗门先生将对公司产生的债务承担个人责任，如同其仍是一名个体经营者。

would have been had he remained a sole trader.

Issue

Is the company which purchased Mr Salomon's previous business fraudulent? Is the company a separate legal person that is distinguishable in law from Mr Salomon?

Judicial View

The first instance judges and the Court of Appeal favoured the liquidator in which both judgments found that the company was in fact acting abnormally and outside of its rights.

The first instance judges stated that, while fraud was not established judging from the facts of the case, agency principles were however used to assert that the company was acting as an agent on behalf of Mr Salomon and he was in turn ordered to indemnify the company for the debts that was incurred while acting as his agent.

The Court of Appeal rejected the agent argument and concluded one of its own, where it argued that the company was acting as a trustee of Mr Salomon who was then the beneficiary. According to Lindley LJ, the company was *"A trustee improperly brought into existence by him to enable him to do what the statute prohibits."* Lopes LJ further argued that the family members who subscribed to the company were *"dummies"* and not bona fide members as the Companies Act 1862 required. This decision held that Mr Salomon,

争议焦点

收购所罗门先生之前业务的公司是否存在欺诈？该公司是否为一家在法律上可与所罗门先生区分开来的独立法人？

司法观点

一审法官和上诉法院均支持了清算人，两份判决中均认为该公司实际上行事异常且超出了其权利范围。

一审法官指出，尽管从案件事实来看，欺诈行为并未得到证实，但是可以用代理人原则来确定该公司是代表所罗门先生行事，于是判令所罗门先生赔偿公司因作为其代理人所产生的债务。

上诉法院驳回了代理人的论点并得出了自己的结论，认为该公司是所罗门先生的受托人，而所罗门先生是受益人。根据林德利法官的说法，该公司属于“**他不正当地创建以使他能从事法规禁止事项的受托人**”。洛佩斯法官进一步认为，认购该公司的家庭成员均是“**傀儡**”，并非《1862 年公司法》要求的善意成员。这个判决命令作为受益人的所罗门先生必须对作为其受托人的公司进行赔偿。

acting as the beneficiary must indemnify the company as his trustee.

However, the essence of this Case came from the House of Lords decision, and will be outlined in more details below:

The House of Lords Decision:

Lord Halsbury:

Lord Halsbury began with a strict approach which focused on the meaning and powers of the Companies Act 1862 (hereinafter referred to as "the Act"). He stated in his judgment, "*the important question in this case, I am not certain it is not the only question, is whether the respondent company was a company at all.*" Lord Halsbury mentioned that the provisions of the Act were of upmost importance and should be applied in the absence of over-complicated considerations on intention. He also contended that the learned judges were confused and therefore were blinded to the fact that the most essential consideration to the case was whether the company in question was ever legitimately constituted. Lord Halsbury went on to confirm that according to the Act, if one becomes a shareholder, he/she would be shareholder for all purposes, meaning that the arguments and doubts as to the true motive behind the subscriptions of the 6 family members are largely irrelevant.

然而，本案的精髓来自上议院的判决，下面将更详细地阐述：

上议院判决：

哈斯伯瑞首席大法官：

哈斯伯瑞大法官从一种严谨的角度展开其论述，聚焦于《1862年公司法》（以下简称该法）的含义和权力。他在判决中指出："我不确定这是不是唯一的问题，但是这个案件的重要问题是去判定被告公司是否真的是一个公司。"哈斯伯瑞大法官提到，该法的规定十分重要，应当在排除对主观意图过度复杂化考量的前提下进行适用。他还提到，博学的法官们产生了困惑，因而无法看到这个案件最核心的考量因素，即被质疑的公司是否曾被合法设立。哈斯伯瑞大法官进一步确认，根据该法，如果一个人成为股东，他/她将在各种意义和层面上成为股东，这意味着关于6位家庭成员认购的真正动机的争论和疑问在很大程度上是无关的。

Denial of the Court of Appeal and first instance argument:

Lord Halsbury rejected the Court of Appeal argument that the formation of the company was a mere sham to allow Mr Salomon to carry out his old business with limited liability and the first instance judgment that the company was an agent of Mr Salomon:

"*I can only find the true intent and meaning of the Act from the Act itself; and the Act appears to me to give a company a legal existence with, as I have said, rights and liabilities of its own, whatever may have been the ideas or schemes of those who brought it into existence.*" Here Lord Halsbury argued that there were only two available outcomes as to whether the company was legitimately constituted, if it was, there should not be considerations on the connection between the company and Mr Salomon as it would be a separate legal person, if it was not, then there would be no person or thing to be agent in the first place.

Lord Halsbury also utilized a principle laid down in another case, *Erlanger v. New Sombrero Phosphate Co3 App. Cas. 1218* in which it was proposed that, "*Persons who purchase property and then create a company to purchase from them the property they possess, stand in a fiduciary position towards that company, and must faithfully state to the company the facts which apply to the property*". Lord Halsbury was satisfied that the family members of Mr Salomon, including himself knew exactly the true state of the facts.

对上诉法院和一审判决理由的否定：

哈斯伯瑞大法官驳回了上诉法院的观点，即公司的设立只是一个让所罗门先生以有限责任继续经营其原业务的虚假行为，以及一审判决中的观点，即公司是所罗门先生的代理人：

“我只能从法案本身找到法案的真实意图和含义；在我看来，法案赋予了公司合法的存在，无论那些使其成立的人的想法或计划是什么，其都拥有自己的权利和义务。”哈斯伯瑞大法官在此指出，关于公司是否合法成立只有两种可能的结果，如果合法，那么就不应该去考虑公司和所罗门先生之间的联系，因为它将是一个独立的法人；如果不合法，则起初就没有人或事物可以作为代理人。

哈斯伯瑞大法官还引用了另一个案件中体现的原则，即厄兰格诉新草帽磷酸盐公司案（3 App. Cas. 1218）中提到的：“个人购买财产后创建公司，并且用其购买了自己原本拥有的财产，他将对该公司存在受托地位并且必须如实向公司陈述与财产有关的事实。”哈斯伯瑞大法官确信，所罗门先生的家庭成员，包括他自己，均非常清楚事实的真实状况。

Lord Watson:

An important statement by Lord Watson concerned the knowledge and potential obligations of the company and its unpaid creditors. Lord Watson submitted that the while the unfortunate position of the creditors were attributed by the Court of Appeal and First instance judges to the appellant (Mr Salomon), the Act casts upon them the duty to be familiar with the state of the company and the information of these matters. He also went on to state that the law does not conform obligations on companies who are struggling with trade to inform the creditors of the potential circumstances that they would unable to be paid.

Lord Macnaghten:

Lord Macnaghten began with a different approach compared to his former judges. He analyzed the facts of the case and deducted the purpose behind Mr Salomon's decision to transform his sole trader business into a limited company, where Lord Macnaghten argued he did so in consideration of his family and that before becoming a limited company, his business was always striving.

After a brief account of the facts, Lord Macnaghten reaffirmed and elaborated on Lord Halsbury's judgment and analysis on the significance of statutes. Lord Macnaghten stated, "*There is nothing in the Act requiring that the subscribers to the memorandum should be independent or unconnected*". This can be understood to mean

沃特森大法官：

沃特森大法官陈述了一项重要的观点，即涉及该公司及其未清偿债权人的了解义务和潜在义务。沃特森大法官提出，虽然上诉法院和一审法官将债权人不幸的境况归因于上诉人（所罗门先生），但法律规定债权人有义务了解公司的状态和该等事项的信息。他还进一步指出，法律并未将通知债权人可能无法得到偿还的潜在情形这一义务强加给经营困难的公司。

麦克纳顿大法官：

麦克纳顿大法官开始论述的角度与前几位法官有所不同。他分析了案件的事实并推断出所罗门先生将自己的个体经营者业务转变为有限公司背后的目的。麦克纳顿大法官认为，他这样做是考虑到他的家庭。在成为有限公司之前，他的业务一直在积极发展。

在简要说明了事实后，麦克纳顿大法官重新确认并详细阐述了哈斯伯瑞大法官关于法规重要性的判断和分析。麦克纳顿大法官指出，“**该法案并未要求公司组织大纲的签署者必须是独立的或互不相关的**”。这可以理解为，所罗门先生与他的家庭成员获得的股票量有明显差别这一事实背后的意图，正如一位

that the intention behind the fact that a bulk of shares were issued to Mr Salomon while his family members received significantly less shares was not a significant factor to hold Mr Salomon liable for using his family members and "*dummies*", as one of the learned judges had stated. Lord Macnaghten also reaffirmed the separate legal persons principle where he stated, "*The company is at law a different person altogether from the subscribers to the memorandum.*"

Lord Davey:

As the final dissenting judge, Lord Davey again rejected the opinions of the lower courts and offered clarity on how this case should have been dealt with had actual fraudulence been involved.

Lord Davey expressed his confusion on the conclusions reached by the lower courts which stated the company in question was acting as an agent or trustee for Mr Salomon. He claimed that there were no express trusts created and no clear equity to support an implied or constructive trust. Lord Davey also contended that the proper course of action that would be utilized in dealing with companies being formed with an unlawful purpose was to invalidate the certificate of incorporation and treat is as a nullity. However, since none of these grounds were able to be pursued and the company, under all the provisions of the Act, was a legitimate entity, no liability can be found on Mr Salomon as he is separate from the company in law.

博学的法官所说，并不是一个重要的足以导致所罗门先生因使用他的家庭成员为“**傀儡**”而承担责任的因素。麦克纳顿大法官也再次确认了法人独立性原则，他指出，“**从法律角度来看，公司与公司组织大纲的签署者完全是不同的人**”。

戴维大法官：

作为最后一位对一审与上诉法院判决持反对意见的法官，戴维大法官再次驳回了下级法院的意见，并对如果涉及实际欺诈本案应如何处理提供了清晰的解释。

戴维大法官对下级法院得出的本案公司是所罗门先生的代理人或受托人的结论表示困惑。戴维大法官认为其中没有明确创建的信托，也没有明确的权益来支持存在暗示或推定的信托。戴维大法官还认为，处理以非法目的成立的公司的正确行动方式应是取消公司的注册证书，并将其视为无效。然而，本案并无可以追究的上述基础，并且公司在该法的所有规定下是合法的，因为所罗门先生在法律上与公司是分开的，无法找到其应承担的责任。

Overall the judges in the House of Lords reached a unanimous decision which rejected the lower courts' attempt to connect the company with Mr Salomon and ultimately held that the company had a separate legal personality and its liability and monetary debts were not to be paid by Mr Salomon.

Comments

The decision reached by the House of Lords critically affirmed the principle of Separate Corporate Personality and with its focus on Statutes, arrived at the conclusion that if a company was formed in compliance with the relevant statutes, its separate legal personality and its separate rights and debts are not to be challenged.

Salomon's confirmation of the SLP principle and its recognition of the ability of a sole trader to transfer his business into a registered limited company and therefore insulating himself from its liabilities remains relevant even today, though it is not without its controversies.

Overall the Salmon v A Salomon Co Ltd case provided the clearest opinion on the principle of separate legal personality and how it operates in practice, which has created a valuable but controversial precedent in not just English, but the entire common law system. However, it is important to bear in mind that the separate personality principle has been the subject of much criticism where it was criticized for being too strict and allows too easily the exploitation by shareholders who are unwilling to bear liabilities.

综上所述，上议院的法官们作出了一致的决定，驳回了下级法院试图将公司与所罗门先生联系起来的尝试，并最终判决该公司具有独立的法律人格，其责任和金钱债务不应由所罗门先生偿还。

案件评述

上议院的决定批判性地肯定了公司法律人格独立的原则，聚焦于法规而得出结论，即如果公司按照相关法规成立，那么其独立的法人地位、独立的权利和债务不应受到挑战。

所罗门案确认了 SLP 原则，并承认了一位个体经营者通过将他的个人业务转变为一家有限公司而将自己与公司的责任隔离的能力。该判决至今仍然重要，但是它也存在争议。

总而言之，所罗门诉所罗门有限责任公司案，对独立法律人格原则以及它在实践中的运作提供了最为清晰的意见。不仅在英国，在整个普通法系中均是有价值但具有争议的先例。然而，我们必须牢记，独立法律人格原则一直受到很多批判，很多人认为这个原则过于严格，且过于容易被意图逃避责任的股东所滥用。

Case 2 Adams v Cape Industries plc

—Establishment of "Piercing (Lifting) the corporate veil"

Preface:

The separate legal personality principle was discussed extensively in the previous case, which explained that a company is distinct in law from its shareholders. It is inevitable that such rule would carry criticisms and areas in need of reconsideration. The courts have long contested and debated the possibility of looking behind the company and discovering that the real "perpetrator" is a dishonest shareholder, or a parent company. This would encourage the court, under certain factual situations to disregard the separate personality principle and hold them liable for the wrongdoings of their subsidiaries. Such an action is often referred to in Common Law as "*Piercing (Lifting) the corporate veil.*"

As the name suggests, piercing the corporate veil allows the courts to rule that the company in question is merely an alter ego used by the shareholders to conceal their dishonest actions, thereby

案例 2　亚当斯诉开普公司案
——“刺破（揭开）公司面纱”的确立

引言：

前一个案例较为广泛地讨论了公司独立法人原则，阐释了公司在法律上与其股东相互独立。该原则不可避免地会遭受批评，存在需要重新考虑的空间。长期以来，法院一直对调查公司背后真正的“肇事者”为不诚实的股东或母公司的可能性提出质疑和辩论。这鼓励了法院在特定情况下无视独立法人原则，并要求他们为其子公司的不当行为承担责任。这种行为在普通法中通常被称为“刺破（揭开）公司面纱”。

顾名思义，当一家公司的面纱被刺破，法院可以裁定，涉案公司只是股东用来掩盖其不诚实行为从而利用独立法人原则逃避责任的另一个“自我”。然而，像独立法人原则这样具体

exploiting the separate legal personality principle to escape liability. However, a principle as concrete and complex as the Separate Legal Personality principle should not be easily defeated, which presented the courts in the United Kingdom one major complication: When can the corporate veil be pierced?

The instances where the court would allow the piercing of the corporate veil have seen much development through history, and this article aims to discuss the first major case which established the occasions where the courts were willing to disregard the separate legal personality.

Facts

A number of class actions were brought by US workers who worked for subsidiary companies within the Cape corporate group ("Cape") in England and sustained injury after extensive exposure to a substance called "asbestos" mined in South Africa. The company which marketed asbestos in the US was called NAAC, which was subsequently went into liquidation and formed two subsidiaries, A.M.C. and C.P.C., all under Cape. The Texan court awarded the judgment in favour of the US workers and against A.M.C. and C.P.C.

Due to the fact that Cape is an English based company, the affair was transferred to the English courts to determine whether Cape would be liable for the tortious activities done by its subsidiaries. To put it plainly, it matters whether the corporate veil may be lifted and the companies which were originally separate

而复杂的原则并不应该轻易被推翻，这也给英国法院带来了一个重大的复杂问题：公司面纱在什么情况下可以被刺破？

法院允许刺破公司面纱的实例，在历史上已经有了长足发展，本文旨在讨论法院同意应无视独立法人原则的第一个重大案例。

案件事实

在英国开普企业集团（以下简称开普公司）旗下子公司工作的美国工人们提起了多起集体诉讼，他们因大量接触南非开采的“石棉”物质而受伤。在美国销售石棉的公司名为NAAC，该公司随后进入清算，并成立了A.M.C. 和 C.P.C. 两家子公司，两家子公司均隶属于开普公司。得克萨斯州法院作出了有利于美国工人方而不利于 A.M.C. 和 C.P.C. 的判决。

由于开普公司是一家英国公司，该事件被移交给了英国法院以确定开普公司是否应对其子公司的侵权活动负责。简单地说，英国法院需要确定是否可以揭开公司面纱，最初合法独立的公司是否存在法律上的关联 。

legally could be in law connected.

Issue

1. Is Cape Industries vicariously liable for the wrongdoings of A.M.C. and C.P.C.?

2. Under what circumstances can the corporate veil be pierced?

Judicial View

Court of Appeal:

In sections of the judgment where piercing of the corporate veil was concerned, Slade J carefully examined the three arguments, namely the "single economic unit" argument, the "façade" argument and the "justice" argument.

The "single economic unit" argument:

Slade J began with a citation from The Albazero [1977] A.C. 774, where Roskil L.J expressly stated that *"each company in a group of companies is a separate legal entity possessed of separate legal rights and liabilities."* What then was left for the court to decide was whether it would be necessary judging from the facts of this case to look behind (Piercing the veil) the separate legal entities to uncover the reality as to how the company (A.M.C., C.P.C. and Cape) functions, meaning if the subsidiaries are wholly owned and

争议焦点

1. 开普公司是否对 A.M.C. 和 C.P.C. 的不当行为承担替代责任？

2. 法院在什么情况下才能刺破公司面纱？

司法观点

上诉法院：

斯雷德法官在判决书中涉及刺破公司面纱的部分，谨慎地分析了三个主要论点，即“单一经济体”论点、“假象”论点和“公正”论点。

“单一经济体”论点：

斯雷德法官一开始引用了奥巴泽若（Albazero [1977] A.C.774）这一案例，其中罗斯基尔大法官明确表示，“**公司集团中的每一家公司都是一个独立的法律实体，拥有独立的法律权利和责任**”。那么留给本案上诉法院予以决定的是，基于本案事实，是否有必要从独立的法律实体背后（刺破面纱）来揭示公司（A.M.C.、C.P.C. 和开普公司）如何运作。这意味着如果子公司是全资子公司，并且完全按照母公司的指示行事，它们也许可被视为同一个经济体。

act exactly as it was directed by the parent company, they may be considered as one economic unit.

Slade J referenced a multiplicity of cases where piercing the corporate veil was duly considered and subsidiaries were contested as to whether they are one with the parent company. First, he cited Lord Simonds in Meyer [1959] A.C. 324, *"In my view, the section warrants the court in looking at the business realities of a situation and does not confine them to a narrow legalistic view."* Here Lord Simonds encouraged the rest of the judges to disregard, to an extent the legal requirement of separate legal personality when it is discovered that in reality, *"every step taken by the subsidiary was determined by the policy of the parent company."*

Following the careful evaluation of the previous cases, Slade J approached the present case, where he stated, *"the court is entitled, indeed bound, to investigate the relationship between the parent and the subsidiary."* After the facts were analyzed, Slade J believed that *"our law, for better or worse, recognises the creation of subsidiary companies, which though in one sense the creatures of their parent companies, will nevertheless under the general law fall to be treated as separate legal entities with all the rights and liabilities which would normally attach to separate legal entities."* The court didn't support the argument that A.M.C. and C.P.C. are in one economic unit with Cape industries.

The "façade" argument:

Slade J moved on from the single economic unit point

斯雷德法官提到了许多案例，在这些案例中，法院适当地考虑了刺破公司面纱的可能性，并对子公司是否与母公司是一家公司提出了质疑。他引用了西蒙兹大法官在梅耶案（[1959] A.C.324）中的论点，“在我看来，该条款要求法院审视商业现实，而非将其局限于狭隘的法律规定”。在这里，西蒙兹大法官鼓励其他法官在一定程度上无视独立法人这一原则，因为在梅耶这一案例的事实中，“子公司迈出的每一步都是由母公司的政策决定的”。

仔细评估了之前的案件后，斯雷德法官处理了本案，他表示，“法院有权，实际上有义务，调查母公司和子公司之间的关系”。在对事实进行分析后，斯雷德法官认为，“我们的法律，无论好坏，均承认在一般法律下，子公司的设立，尽管在某种意义上是其母公司的产物，仍将被视为独立的法律实体，并拥有通常附属于独立法律实体的所有权利和责任”。法院没有支持 A.M.C. 和 C.P.C. 与开普公司系同一个经济体的论点。

“假象”论点：

斯雷德法官结束了单一经济体的观点，并转向了“只有在

and turned to the argument that *"it is appropriate to pierce the corporate veil only where special circumstances exist indicating that it is a mere façade concealing the true facts."* The diction of the word "façade" is intricate as it suggests that the company may be using their subsidiaries as a cover to hide their participation in the wrongdoing.

Slade J opened his analysis with the statement, *"whenever a device or sham or cloak is alleged in cases such as this, the motive of the alleged perpetrator must be legally relevant."* After careful consideration, Slade J expressed his view on the intention behind the liquidation of N.A.A.C and the creation of A.M.C. and C.P.C., where he inferred to be: enabling sales of asbestos from the South African subsidiaries to continue to be made in the UK while reducing their appearance of involvement and the risk of any subsidiary or of Cape as parent company being held liable for US taxation.

With the interpreted intention at hand, Slade J proceeded to consider whether the said intentions were enough to constitute a façade and as a result justify the piercing of the corporate veil.

Slade J considered the argument submitted by the plaintiff (victims of asbestos poisoning)'s lawyer which stated that the courts will lift the veil in situations where the company is trying to evade: (i) limitations imposed on his conduct by law; (ii) such rights of relief against him as third parties already possess; and (iii) such rights of relief as third parties may in the future acquire. While Slade J decided in this case that there is no evidence which indicates

特殊情况下，即公司只是为了掩盖事实的幌子时，才可以刺破公司的面纱”这一论点。“假象”一词的措辞很复杂，因为它表明该公司可能利用其子公司作为掩护，从而掩盖其参与不法行为的证据。

斯雷德法官在分析开始时说，“**当在此类案件中存在有不当手段、骗局或掩盖事实等指控时，被指控者的动机均具有法律相关性**”。斯雷德法官经过仔细考虑表达了他对开普公司在 N.A.A.C. 的清算以及创建 A.M.C. 和 C.P.C. 的背后意图的看法。他推断出的意图为：在减少其参与的证据以及任何子公司或母公司开普公司所承担的美国税收风险的同时，使南非子公司的石棉销售能够继续在英国进行。

有了对意图的解析之后，斯雷德法官开始考虑上述意图是否足以构成一个假象，从而证明刺破公司面纱的合理性。

斯雷德法官考虑了原告（石棉中毒受害者）律师提出的论点，该论点指出，在公司试图逃避以下三点的情况下，法院将揭开面纱：（1）逃避法律对其行为施加的限制；（2）逃避第三方已经拥有的针对他的赔偿权利；以及（3）逃避第三方将来可能获得的赔偿权利。虽然斯雷德法官在本案中决定开普公司的运作中并不存在上述三个因素，但他同时认识到该三点验证标准的明确性和可行性，该标准可能在未来的案件中使用。

that Cape industries is liable for the three factors stated above, he did recognize the clarity and feasibility of this test, which may be used in future cases.

Slade J gathered the details of this case (here omitted) and gave out the judgment that N.A.A.C. was carrying on business of its own, and not acting as a mere façade covering for Cape.

The "justice" argument:

The justice argument stated that in certain circumstances the court should pierce the corporate veil simply because it was "just" to do so. The appellant side argued that in cases where not piercing the corporate veil will produce injustice, the court ought to avoid such misfortunes. However, this argument was rejected by Slade J, where he stated, *"save in cases which turn on the wording of particular statutes or contracts, the court is not free to disregard the principle of Salomon v A Salomon & Co Ltd [1897] AC 22 merely because it considers that justice so requires."*

Comments

The various judgments and theories cited in this case may be interpreted to focus on one element, which is "control". The more control the parent company has on the subsidiary, the more likely it is for them to be recognised as one economic unit.

The significance of this case should not be overshadowed by the court rejecting to lift the corporate veil, but instead its value lies

斯雷德法官收集了本案的细节（此处省略），并作出判决，即 N.A.A.C. 在进行自己的业务，而不是开普公司用来遮盖事实的假象。

“公正”论点：

“公正”论点指出，在某些情况下，法院应该仅仅因为这样做是“公正的”，从而刺破公司的面纱。上诉方辩称，法庭应该避免这种拒绝刺破公司面纱从而产生不公正的不幸情况。然而，斯雷德法官驳回了这一论点，他表示，“除了涉及特定法规或合同措辞的案件外，法院不能仅仅因为认为公正需要，就随意无视所罗门诉所罗门有限公司案（[1897]AC 22）的原则”。

案件评述

本案中引用的各种判决和理论可以被理解为均集中在一个要素上，即“控制权”。母公司对子公司的控制权越多，法院就越有可能将其视为同一个经济体。

本案不应因法院拒绝刺破公司面纱而失去重要性，相反，其作用在于其制定了许多标准和原则。在不同的情况下，这些

in the many tests and principles created which may, under different circumstances, encourage the court to pierce the corporate veil. Though one must consider, after reading this case, the position of Slade J was clear in expressing that in future cases only the façade argument may be powerful enough to encourage the relevant courts to pierce the corporate veil. The justice and the single economic unit argument may not be of much relevance.

With that being said, the three main arguments, (justice, façade and single economic unit) lasted for nearly a quarter of a century unchallenged and devoid of reforms, until a significant case in 2013 created two new principles in discussing the piercing of the corporate veil which we will discuss in next case.

标准和原则可能会鼓励法院刺破公司的面纱。但是在阅读了本案后，人们必须考虑到，斯雷德法官的立场是明确的。他表示，在未来的案件中，只有“假象”论点可能足以使得相关法院刺破公司的面纱。“公正”和“单一经济体”的论点可能没有太大的相关性。

话虽如此，“公正”“假象”“单一经济体”这三个主要论点持续了近 25 年且没有受到质疑或改革，直到 2013 年的一个重大案件在讨论刺破公司面纱时产生了两项新原则，我们将在下一篇案例中讨论这两项原则。

Case 3 Prest v Petrodel Resources Ltd

—Latest development of "Piercing (Lifting) the corporate veil"

Preface:

The three principles (single economic unit, façade and justice) identified and examined in the last article stood authoritative for 23 years without significant improvements, until in 2013 when Lord Sumption at the Supreme Court in Prest reimagined the rules regarding the piercing of the corporate veil.

Lord Sumption identified two distinct principles: The concealment and the evasion principle. However, he later argued that the concealment principle does not involve the piercing of the corporate personality but simply an act of looking behind the companies to see who is there. As a result, this article will focus mainly on the evasion principle, which remains today as one of the authoritative justifications on piercing the corporate veil.

案例3　普雷斯特诉派绰德资源有限公司案
——“刺破（揭开）公司面纱”的最新发展

引言：

上篇文章指出和分析的三项原则（单一经济体、假象和公正）在23年内一直具有权威性且无重大发展。直到2013年，普雷斯特案中的撒姆逊大法官重新构想了有关刺破公司面纱的规则。

撒姆逊大法官提出了两个截然不同的原则：隐瞒原则和逃避原则。然而，他后来认为，隐瞒原则并不涉及对公司人格的刺穿，而只是去观察并发现隐藏在公司背后的操控者。因此，本文将重点探讨逃避原则，这一原则至今仍然是刺破公司面纱的权威理由之一。

Facts

Prest concerns the divorcing couple, Mr and Mrs Prest, and the question whether Mrs Prest could legally obtain monetary properties of her husband through matrimonial settlement, governed by the Matrimonial Causes Act 1973. Section 24(1)(a) of the Act stated: "*A court may order that a party to the marriage shall transfer to the other party, such property as may be so specified, being property to which the first- mentioned party is entitled, either in possession or reversion.*" Mrs Prest argued that her husband's wealth vastly exceeded what he declared and that a majority of his wealth are stored in many of his companies, which consequently included both Mr Prest and his company Petrodel Resources Ltd. as respondents to the claim. The court had to consider whether it was justifiable following the facts of this case to pierce the corporate veil and declare the pecuniary properties in question belonging not solely to the company, but also to her husband.

The first instance court (Family Division) examined the facts of the case carefully and passed the judgment that since Mr Prest has been managing the companies' affairs solely for his benefit and had clearly used them to meet his and his family's personal expenditure, as well as his legal costs in the instant proceedings, the assets held by the companies are in reality his. The first instance court held that Petrodel Resources Ltd was liable and must pay Mrs Prest the assets equivalent to 17.5 million (half of the company's assets) that she was legally entitled.

案件事实

普雷斯特案涉及离婚夫妇普雷斯特先生和普雷斯特夫人，以及普雷斯特夫人是否可以通过《1973年婚姻诉讼法》中规定的婚姻和解法获得丈夫的金钱财产。该法第24（1）（a）条规定："**法院可命令婚姻的一方向另一方转移指定的财产，即第一方有权拥有或收回的财产。**"普雷斯特夫人称，她丈夫的财富远超他所声明的部分，而且他的大部分财富都储存在他的许多公司中，因此，普雷斯特先生和他的公司——派绰德资源有限公司——都是该索赔的被告。法院必须考虑，根据本案的事实，是否有正当理由刺破公司面纱，宣布所涉金钱财产不仅属于公司，而且属于她的丈夫。

一审法院（家事法庭）仔细审查了案件事实后作出判决，由于普雷斯特先生一直只为自己的利益管理公司事务，并显然用此支付他和家人的个人开支以及他在此诉讼中的法律费用，这些公司持有的资产实际属于他所有。一审法院认为，派绰德资源有限公司负有责任，必须向普雷斯特女士支付其合法拥有的资产，即1750万英镑（公司财产的一半）。

The appellant companies appealed against the decision in an effort to overturn the financial order made in favour of Mrs Prest. The judge in the Court of Appeal allowed the appeal and held that a company's assets belong beneficially to the company itself and not to its shareholders, and the fact that the assets were controlled by one single shareholder (Mr Prest) made no difference to the separate legal personality principle set out in Salomon v A Salmon & Co Ltd.

Mrs Prest appealed the decision made by the Court of Appeal and as the decision reached the Supreme Court, the leading judgment was given by Lord Sumption.

Issue

Under what circumstances can the properties owned by a company declared to also be owned by the shareholder, in turn justifying the piercing of the corporate veil?

Judicial View

The concealment principle:

The concealment principle, as argued by Lord Sumption is, to a great extent, similar to the façade argument in *Adams v Cape*, which involves, quote: *"not disregarding the 'facade', but only looking behind it to discover the facts which the corporate structure is concealing."*[1]

[1] Adams v Cape Industries, plc [1990] Ch 433 (CA).

该公司对一审法院的裁决提出上诉，并试图推翻有利于普雷斯特夫人的支付指令。上诉法院的法官支持了上诉请求，认为公司的资产属于公司本身，而不是属于其股东。资产由一名单一股东（普雷斯特先生）控制的事实并不会影响所罗门诉所罗门有限公司案中规定的独立法人原则。

普雷斯特夫人对上诉法院的裁决提出上诉，随着裁决到达最高法院，撒姆逊大法官作出了主要判决。

争议焦点

在何种情况下，公司所拥有的财产才能被宣布为亦是其股东的财产，从而证明刺破公司面纱是正当的？

司法观点

隐瞒原则：

撒姆逊大法官所主张的隐瞒原则在很大程度上类似于亚当斯诉开普公司案中的假象论点，其中引用了一句话：“**并不是忽视‘假象’，而只是从背后寻找隐瞒公司结构的事实。**”[1]撒姆逊大法官后来提出，隐瞒原则并不涉及刺破开公司面纱，而

[1] 亚当斯诉开普公司案，[1990] Ch 433 (CA)。

Lord Sumption later submitted that the concealment principle does not involve the piercing of the corporate veil, but simply taking a deeper glance at the structure of the company. Therefore, the focus of the judgment was the evasion principle.

The evasion principle:

Similar to Slade J in *Adams v Cape*, Lord Sumption cited a huge amount of case laws where the evasion principle may have been used, and from the judgments he derived the essence of the evasion principle.

Lord Sumption began with an older case, *Gilford Motor Co Ltd v Horne[1933] Ch 935*, where Mr Horne in the case was precluded from engaging in any competing business in the specified area for five years after the end of his previous employment. Though he later, within five years formed a company named after his wife. Lord Hanworth MR stated that the company was a *"mere cloak of sham"* since the business was in reality carried mainly by Mr Horne. On the surface this may seem like a case where the concealment principle was in use, though it was in Lord Sumption's opinion that the court in Gilford Motor Co Ltd was really applying the evasion principle. Lord Sumption cited Lawrence LJ, where in his judgment the company in question was *"a mere channel used by the defendant Horne for the purpose of enabling him, for his own benefit, to obtain the advantage of the customers of the plaintiff company, and that therefore the defendant company ought to be restrained as well as the defendant Horne."* Lord Sumption

只是更深入地审视公司的结构。因此，此案判决的重点是逃避原则。

逃避原则：

与亚当斯诉开普公司案中的斯莱德法官相似，撒姆逊大法官列举了大量可能使用了逃避原则的案例，并从这些判决中得出了逃避原则的精华。

撒姆逊大法官从一个较老的案件开始分析，即吉尔福德汽车公司诉霍恩案（[1933] Ch 935）。该案中，霍恩先生被要求在前一份工作结束后的5年内不得在指定区域从事任何竞争性业务。然而，他后来在5年内成立了一个以他妻子的名字命名的公司。汉沃斯大法官在此案中表示，该公司“只是一个伪装”，因为该公司业务实际上主要是由霍恩经营。从表面上看，这似乎是一个使用了隐瞒原则的案件，但是撒姆逊大法官认为，吉尔福德汽车公司这个案件中的法院实际上运用了逃避原则。撒姆逊大法官引用了劳伦斯大法官在其判决中的主张：所涉公司“仅是被告霍恩出于其自身利益而获取原告公司的有利客户资源的渠道，因此，被告公司应与被告霍恩一起受到约束”。撒姆逊大法官表示，本案正确地适用了逃避原则。

delivered that the case presented a correct application of the evasion principle.

To demonstrate the full appearance of the evasion principle, Lord Sumption cited cases where the evasion principle was applied incorrectly. In *Trustor AB v Smallbone (No 2) [2001] 1 WLR 1177*, Mr Smallbone's company received funds from Turstor AB on behalf of him, which led to the judge stating that the corporate veil may be pierced if the company was used as a *"device or facade to conceal the true facts thereby avoiding or concealing any liability of those individual(s)."* In this analysis by the judge both the evasion and the concealment principles were mentioned, though Lord Sumption, after citing this case held the opinion that in fact none of the principle were in use. He argued that in this case the corporate veil was not pierced at all, since the judgment was simply an application of the rule that *"receipt by a company will count as receipt by the shareholder if the company received it as his agent or nominee."* This said rule was the ultimate reason which led to the decision that the money was in fact received by Mr Smallbone, but not the evasion principle nor the concealment principle.

Lord Sumption's reference to cases which correctly applied the evasion principle and cases that did not formed his position on the future of the evasion principle: *"I conclude that there is a limited principle of English law which applies when a person is under an existing legal obligation or liability or subject to an existing legal restriction which he deliberately evades or whose enforcement he deliberately frustrates by interposing a company under his control."*

为了完整地展示逃避原则，撒姆逊大法官列举了逃避原则应用不当的案例。在信托人AB诉斯莫伯恩（No 2）案（[2001] 1 WLR 1177）中，斯莫伯恩先生的公司代表他从信托人AB处收到资金，这导致法官指出，如果公司被用作“掩盖真实事实的手段或伪装，从而避免或隐瞒个人的任何责任”，则公司的面纱可能被刺破。在这位法官的分析中提到了逃避和隐瞒原则，但是撒姆逊大法官在引用该案后认为，实际上没有任何一项原则在本案中被使用。他辨析道，本案中，公司面纱根本没有被刺破，因为判决只是适用了“如果公司作为其代理人或被提名人收到资金，则公司收到的资金被视为股东收到”这一规则。这一规定是导致认定实际是斯莫伯恩先生收到款项的最终原因，而不是逃避原则或隐瞒原则。

撒姆逊大法官以他提到的这些正确和不正确适用逃避原则的案例，得出了他对这一原则在未来案件中使用的看法：“我的结论是，英国法律有一项有限的原则，应适用于以下情况：当某人承担现有的法律义务或责任，或受现有的法律限制，而此人故意通过其控制的公司的介入而规避该义务或责任，并且阻挠该义务的执行。”撒姆逊大法官认为，在大多数情况下，公司与股东之间存在隐藏的关系，因此没有必要刺破公司的面

It is in Lord Sumption's opinion that in most cases there exists a hidden relationship between the company and the shareholder which renders it unnecessary to pierce the corporate veil. To put it plainly, only when one is deliberately abusing the separate legal personality of a company to evade the law, is it possible to pierce the corporate veil through the evasion principle.

Lord Sumption further argued that in most cases where the courts decided to hold the shareholders liable was merely an act that granted injunctions as an equitable remedy on the ground of tort law, and that in essence the corporate veil was not lifted at all. There exists similarly a high bar on the evasion principle, which signifies that if the principle has been established, some other legal principle has to be applied simultaneously. In the case of Prest, trust principles were utilized, where the judges argued that the properties in question were in fact held by the company on trust for the husband. *"The main, if not the only, reason for the companies' failure to co-operate was to protect the seven properties, which in turn suggested that... accordingly, the seven disputed properties were held by the companies on trust for the husband."* The Supreme Court ultimately allowed the appeal and held that the corporate veil were to be pierced and the companies' assets were to be distributed to Mrs Prest as ordered by the Matrimonial Causes Act 1973.

纱。简短来说，只有故意滥用公司独立法人资格规避法律，才有可能通过逃避原则刺破公司面纱。

撒姆逊大法官进一步论述，在大多数情况下，法院决定追究股东的责任只是一种根据衡平法给予禁令作为公平补救的行为，而从本质上讲，公司的面纱根本没有被揭开。同样，逃避原则的使用也存在很高的标准。这意味着，如果已经确定适用逃避原则，则必须同时适用一些其他法律原则。在普雷斯特案中就采用了信托原则，法官认为，存在争议的有关财产事实上是由公司为丈夫信托持有的。“公司不合作的主要原因（如果不是唯一原因）是为了保护这七项财产，这反过来又表明……这七项有争议的财产由公司以信托形式为丈夫持有。”最高法院最终支持了上诉，并裁定公司的面纱将被刺破，公司的资产将按照《1973年婚姻诉讼法》的规定分配给普雷斯特夫人。

Comments

The main idea to remember following the Prest case was that the courts are extremely unwilling in most circumstances to "pierce the corporate veil". In most cases where the shareholder may be potentially held liable for the wrongdoings or the liabilities of the company, the court will first attempt the discover connections between the shareholders and the company, to look behind the company structure, this, in the judge's opinion does not involve disregarding the separate legal personality rule decided in Salomon v A Salomon Ltd, as it remains the starting point for all similar company law cases and that it is not to be disregarded easily. Furthermore, the judges in Prest contended that in most scenarios the "piercing of the corporate veil" is not a doctrine but a label, a result that must be reached by other legal means, such as the trust principles in Prest.

From the two cases analyzed in the two articles, the judges' position appeared exceedingly apparent that the "piercing of the corporate veil" is not and will very possibly never be a fully established doctrine. Many Judges hold different positions on this matter and it will take an abundance of reforms and effort to formulate the corporate veil principle.

案件评述

普雷斯特案之后要记住的主要观点是，法院在绝大多数情况下都极不愿意“刺破公司面纱”。通常，如果股东可能对公司的错误行为或责任承担责任，法院将首先尝试发现股东与公司之间的联系，以查看公司的背后结构，法官认为，这不涉及无视所罗门诉所罗门有限公司案中确立的独立法人原则，因为它仍然是所有类似公司法案件的起点，且不应被轻易忽视。此外，普雷斯特案中的法官主张，在大多数情境下，“刺破公司面纱”不是一种学说，而是一种标签，且必须通过其他法律手段，如本案中的信托原则，才能达到这一结果。

从这两篇文章分析的两个案例看，法官的立场似乎非常明显，即“刺破公司面纱”不是也很可能永远不会是一个完全确立的学说。许多法官在这个问题上持有不同的立场，制定刺破公司面纱原则仍需要进行大量的改革和努力。

Part Two: Selected Cases under IP Law

Case 1 University of London Press Ltd v University of Tutorial Press Ltd

[1916] 2 Ch 601 (1916)

Case 2 Coco v AN Clark (Engineers) Ltd

[1968] F.S.R. 415

Case 3 Kogan v Martin

[2020] E.C.D.R. 3

第二部分：知识产权法案例

Case 1 University of London Press Ltd v University of Tutorial Press Ltd

—The idea of a literary work and its originality

Preface:

The world of literature as we know it has come a long way from its first creation. The human intellect was gifted the ability of literary creation from the first carvings on the cave walls, to the AI generated novels now 40,000 years later. What differs the modern age for literature from the ancient times is the need of protection for the author of the work, which is now commonly known as: Copyright. The owners of copyrights in the UK have the right to protect their work from persons attempting to benefit or use illegally, and yet the court had long contested the extent of copyright protection and the relevant requirements where a piece of work must follow in order to be protected.

Two of the most controversial and problematic tests to apply are the test of "literary work" and the test of "originality". When is a work "literary"? When can a work be considered "original"? This early English case law may aid in answering these questions.

案例 1 伦敦大学出版社有限公司诉辅导大学出版社有限公司案
——文学作品及其独创性

引言：

从最初的创作开始，我们所知道的文学世界已经走过了漫长的道路。最初的洞窟石刻与 4 万年后的今天人工智能撰写的小说，均是人类智力中文学创作能力的体现。现代文学与古代文学的不同之处，在于保护作品作者的必要性，现在众所周知为：版权。在英国，版权所有者有权保护其作品不受试图非法受益者或非法使用者的侵害，但法院长期以来一直对版权保护的范围和作品为获得保护而应予以遵循的要求提出疑问。

其中，最具争议性和疑问性的两个验证标准是“文学作品”验证标准和“独创性”验证标准。什么情况下一部作品是“文学的”？什么情况下作品才算“原创”？这个早期的英国判例可能有助于回答这两个问题。

Facts

The University of London had appointed two examiners, Professor Lodge and Mr Jackson to co-author the examination papers used for the matriculation exam in the school of mathematics. The examiners were not direct employees of the University, and were free to be appointed by any other Universities. They were also free to choose their own questions, provided that they abided by a syllabus appointed by the University.

There was a resolution by the University which stated all the examination papers authored by the external examiners are intellectual works belonging to the University, and all the relevant copyrights possessed by the examiners would be vested in the University. A while after the examination papers were finalized, the University entered into an agreement with the plaintiff's company, University of London Press Ltd, where it was commonly agreed upon that the plaintiff would acquire all such copyrights and rights of publication from the University of the papers in a schedule, including the matriculation examination papers co-authored by Professor Lodge and Mr Jackson.

After the plaintiff company published the examination papers, the defendant company, the University of Tutorial Press Ltd issued a publication which included a portion of all the matriculation papers in January 1916, which coincidentally included three examination papers authored by Professor Lodge and Mr Jackson. The defendant did not copy directly from the publication of the

案件事实

伦敦大学任命洛奇教授和杰克逊先生两名考官共同撰写数学学院入学考试的试卷。考官并不是大学的直接雇员，且可以被任何其他大学自由任命。只要他们遵守大学指定的教学大纲，他们也可以自由选择如何出题。

校方曾通过一项决议，规定外聘考官撰写的所有试卷均为校方的智力成果，考官拥有的一切相关版权归校方所有。在试卷定稿后不久，大学与原告公司伦敦大学出版社有限公司签订了一项协议，双方一致同意原告将从伦敦大学获得一份附件中所有作品的版权和发表权，其中包括洛奇教授和杰克逊先生合编的入学考试试卷。

在原告公司公布考卷后，被告公司辅导大学出版社有限公司于 1916 年 1 月发布了一份涵盖部分入学考试试卷的出版物，其中碰巧包含洛奇教授和杰克逊先生撰写的三份考卷。被告没有直接抄袭原告公司的出版物，而是从学生提供的副本中取得。该出版物包括试卷、答案和关于考试难度的评论。

plaintiff's company but instead took from the copies provided by students. The publication included the examination papers, along with its answers and words of criticism which commented on the difficulty of the exam.

The Plaintiff company discovered the publication and commenced action against the defendant company for infringement of copyright. Since Professor Lodge and Mr Jackson were the original authors of the papers, they were joined in the proceedings as co-plaintiffs.

Issue

1. What is considered as a literary work?
2. When is a work original?
3. When is copyright infringed?

Judicial View

The Law:

Section 1 of The Copyright Act 1911 states:

"Subject to the provisions of this Act, copyright shall subsist throughout the parts of His Majesty's dominions to which this Act extends for the term hereinafter mentioned in every original literary dramatic musical and artistic work, if—"

The key diction in this section is "literary, dramatic musical and artistic." It is of relevance in the present case whether examination

原告公司发现了该出版物后，以侵犯版权为由对被告公司提起诉讼。由于洛奇教授和杰克逊先生是试卷的原作者，他们作为共同原告加入了诉讼程序。

争议焦点

1. 什么可以被认定为文学作品?
2. 何种情况下一个作品具有独创性?
3. 何种情况下著作权会被侵犯?

司法观点

法律条文:

《1911 年版权法》第 1 条规定:

> 在符合本法规定以及在下述情况下，版权应存在于本法所延伸的英皇陛下的领土范围之内，在每部原创的文学、戏剧、音乐及艺术作品中均应存在……

本条的重点词汇是“文学、戏剧、音乐和艺术”。试卷是否被视为“文学作品”，与本案有较高的关联性。

papers are considered as "literary works".

The arguments for the plaintiffs:

The submissions by the plaintiff company are summarised in the below points:

1. The University owned the copyright to the examination papers since the examiners were employed by the University under a "contract of service" and the works in question were created in the duration of their employment. As a result, the plaintiff company is now the rightful owner of the copyrights since they formed the agreement with the University on the transferring of the right.

2. The examination papers in question were able to be protected under the 1911 Act since they should be included under "literary works". In section 35, subsection 1 of the Act, "Literary works" included "compilations", the examination papers were to be considered as "compilations". The literary work in question were original as they, "*entailed the exercise of brainwork, memory, and trained judgment, and even the selection of passages from other authors' works.*" Following such logics, the defendant company has infringed the copyright belonging to the plaintiff company by producing the examination papers.

The arguments for the defendant:

To respond to the plaintiffs, the defendant argued that the plaintiff company had no copyright since the right could not have

原告的论点：

原告公司提交的论点总结如下：

1. 大学拥有试卷的版权，因为考官是基于“雇佣合同”而受雇于大学，所涉作品是在其任职期间创作。因此，原告公司自与学校签订权利转让协议以来，已成为版权的合法所有人。

2. 本案涉及的试卷可以根据《1911 年版权法》得到保护，因为它们应被列入“文学作品”项下。在该法第 35 条第 1 款中，“文学作品”包括“汇编”，试卷应被视为“汇编”。所讨论的文学作品是原创的，因为它们“需要运用脑力、记忆力和经过训练的判断力，甚至还需要从其他作者的作品中选择段落”。按照这样的逻辑，被告公司因发布试卷而侵犯了原告公司的版权。

被告的论点：

为回应原告，被告辩称，原告公司没有版权，因为考虑到该大学从未从两位作者本人那里获得版权，该权利本来就不可

been transferred to them in the first place, considering that the University never acquired the copyright from the two authors themselves. According to the 1911 Act, the plaintiff company must either be the author, owner, or the assignee of the work. Professor Lodge and Mr Jackson were not under a "contract of service" for the University since they were not direct employees. They were free to perform the work in their own time, and the University did not have direct control over them in any way. The defendant representatives cited case laws which concerned "contract of service" and contended that similar to *Smith v. General Motor Cab Co,* where the taxicab driver was not under a contract of service for the owners of the cab, the University in the present case also holds no contract of service towards the authors.

Two lawyers acting for the defendant further argued, the co-plaintiff examiners also hold no copyright over the examination papers since they could not be considered as "literary works". They submitted, the current 1911 Act on what can be protected sets a higher standard for the definition of "literary works" than what was originally written as "book" in the Copy Right Act 1842. They stated that "literary works" is much narrower of a concept than "book". The examination papers are mere copies of common knowledge already known to man as the work itself comprises of already known ideas, which cannot be considered to be "original". Furthermore, the work was not difficult to compose at all, the creation process did not require much efforts or time from the examiners.

能转让给他们。根据《1911 年版权法》，原告公司必须是作品的作者、所有者或受让人。洛奇教授和杰克逊先生不是直接雇员，与大学并无“雇佣合同”。他们可以在自己的时间里自由地完成工作，大学对他们也没有任何直接的控制权。被告代表援引了有关“雇佣合同”的案例，并主张与史密斯诉通用的士汽车公司案类似，出租车司机在该案中不是与出租车车主公司基于“雇佣合同”的雇员。本案中的大学和两位作者也不存在雇佣关系。

被告的两名律师进一步辩称，作为共同原告的考官们也对试卷不享有著作权，因为它们不能被视为“文学作品”。他们认为，与《1842 年版权法》中最初写为“书”的措辞相比，现行《1911 年版权法》中关于什么可以被保护的内容为“文学作品”的定义设定了更高的标准。他们指出，“文学作品”是一个比“书”更狭义的概念。因为试卷作品本身包括人类已知的想法，试卷仅仅是复制于常识，不能被认为是“独创”的。此外，此试卷作品的创作根本不困难，创作过程中不需要考官付出太多的努力或时间。

Peterson J:

Peterson J analysed the facts of the case and delivered a thorough judgment on what are to be considered as "literary works" and what is the standard for the test of originality.

Literary works:

Peterson J argued that the phrase "literary works" should not be viewed as a form of confinement on the inclusion of works by authors. *"It may be difficult to define 'literary work' as used in this Act, but it seems to be plain that it is not confined to 'literary work' in the sense in which that phrase is applied".* He further stated, *"In speaking of such writings as literary works, one thinks of the quality, the style, and the literary finish which they exhibit."* He provided several examples which had no specific literary style, but could however be considered "literary works", such as a list of foxhounds and hunting days, trade catalogues, and a list of registered bills of sale. Peterson J commented on the defendant's opinion that the current wording is narrower than the past, and stated that the present Act cannot be seen as intending to curtail the rights of authors, therefore the scope could only be extended, not vice versa. He concluded his judgment on this section by stating, *"the words 'literary work' cover work which is expressed in print or writing, irrespective of the question whether the quality or style is high...Papers set by examiners are, in my opinion, 'literary work'*

彼得森法官：

彼得森法官分析了案件的事实，并对什么是“文学作品”以及什么是验证独创性的标准作出了透彻的判断。

文学作品：

彼得森法官认为，“文学作品”一词不应被视为限制作者作品的一种形式。“本法中使用的‘文学作品’可能难以界定，但似乎很明显，它并不局限于‘文学作品’这一用语所适用的意义。”他进一步指出，“把这样的作品称为文学作品，人们会想到它们所表现出来的质量、风格和最终呈现的文学效果”。他提供了数个没有具体文学风格，但可以被视为“文学作品”的例子，如猎狐犬和狩猎日的清单、贸易目录和登记销售票据的清单。彼得森法官对被告的意见作出了评论，即目前的措辞比过去更有局限性，并指出不能将现行法律的意图视为意在限制作者的权利，因此只能扩大范围，而不能反之。他在对这一节的判决进行总结时提到，“‘文学作品’一词涵盖了印刷品或书面作品，无论质量或风格是否高……在我看来，考官撰写的考卷属于本法意义上的‘文学作品’”。

within the meaning of the present Act."

Originality:

As the examination papers have been decided to be literary works, the question which the court must then decide in whether they are "original". What Peterson J opened his judgment on this section with a sentence that is still in use today, after more than a century later, *"The word 'original' does not in this connection mean that the work must be the expression of original or inventive thought. Copyright Acts are not concerned with the originality of ideas, but with the expression of thought."* The distinction between the originality of ideas and expression of thought can be interpreted to mean, that so long as the author takes from the world what already exists and expresses such information in his own way, without copying directly from another work, the work shall be considered "original". The focus should not be the starting point of creation, but rather the process, where the author had contributed his own thoughts and efforts into. Peterson J also commented on the defendant's argument that the examination efforts required little time and efforts to compose, to which he responded, *"If time expended is to be the test, the rapidity of an author like Lord Byron in producing a short poem might be an impediment in the way of acquiring copyright, and, the completer his mastery of his subject, the smaller would be the prospect of the author's success in maintaining his claim to copyright."* Peterson J held that the examination papers had passed the test of originality.

独创性：

由于试卷已被确定为文学作品，法庭必须决定这些试卷是否基于“原创”。彼得森法官在该部分判决的开头使用了一句在一个多世纪之后仍被使用的话语：“‘原创’一词并不意味着作品必须是原初性或创造性思想的表达。版权法关注的不是思想的独创性，而是想法的表达。”思想的独创性和想法的表达之间的区别可以理解为，只要作者从世界上获取已经存在的东西，并以自己的方式表达这些信息，而不直接从另一幅作品中抄袭，该作品就应被视为拥有“独创性”。关注的重点不应该是创作的起点，而是作者为之贡献自己思想和努力的过程。彼得森法官还评论了被告的论点，即编卷工作几乎不需要花费时间和精力来完成。“如果说时间是一种验证标准的话，拜伦勋爵这样的作家创作一首短诗的速度可能会成为获得版权的障碍，而且，他对自己的主题掌握得越透彻，作者成功维护自己的版权主张的可能性就越小。”彼得森法官认定试卷通过了独创性的验证标准。

Ownership and Infringement:

With the two pre-requisites decided, it was left to the court to decide who the legitimate owner of the copyright was and whether there was infringement on the part of the defendant.

Peterson J argued that for the purposes of the 1911 Act, *"the author is the first owner of the copyright, subject only to the exceptions contained in the act."* The exception which was relevant in the present case was the employment relationship between the two authors and the University. Peterson J drew from the relevant facts and stated that since the examiners were not direct employees of the company, were paid only for the specific job they were appointed to complete, and worked freely in their own time and discretion, there exists no "contract of service" between the two parties but was in reality a "contract for service". Under this situation the examiners are the first and sole owners of the copyright.

However, one may remember from the facts that there was a resolution which stated that copy rights of all examination papers were to be transferred to the University. Since the examiners had not assigned the copyright in writing signed by them or their agent, the University was only equitably entitled to the copyright. The agreement formed between the University and the plaintiff company made the company become equitably entitled to the copyright. Since the plaintiffs were only equitably entitled, they could not directly claim for copyright infringement, they must join the original owners in the claim. Peterson J concluded his argument

所有权与侵权：

在这两个先决条件均已确定的情况下，法院需决定版权的合法所有者，以及被告是否存在侵权行为。

彼得森法官认为，就《1911 年版权法》的立法目的而言，“**仅限于法案中包含的例外情况，作者是版权的第一所有者**”。与本案有关的例外情况是两名作者与大学之间的雇佣关系。彼得森法官从相关事实中得出结论，并表示由于考官不是公司的直接员工，只为他们被指定完成的特定工作支付报酬，并且在他们自己的时间和自由裁量权内自由工作，双方之间不存在“雇佣合同”关系，而实际上是“服务合同”关系。在这种情况下，考官是版权的第一和唯一所有者。

不过，我们可能记得案件事实中有一项决议，规定所有试卷版权均要转到大学所有。由于考官或其代理人没有以书面形式签署而将版权转让，大学只有在衡平法下享有权益。大学与原告公司之间达成的协议使该公司享有衡平法下的权益。由于原告只有衡平法下权益，他们不能直接提出侵犯版权的索赔。原告公司必须与原所有者一起提出索赔。彼得森法官在关于所有权的论点的最后指出，由于两名考官被列为共同原告，原告公司在法律上可以主张版权被侵犯。

on ownership by stating that since the two examiners were included as co-plaintiffs, the plaintiff company was legally able to claim copyright infringement.

Finally, Peterson J considered the defendant's submission that they published the work under the "fair dealing" rule and were only publishing the work for the purposes of private study, which was a purpose allowed explicitly in the Act. Drawing upon the facts, Peterson J held that since the relevant works were already published once by the plaintiff company, and the defendant company had not added enough novel information to achieve their said purpose, the defendant company had infringed the plaintiff company's copyright.

Comments

The present case remains one of the leading case laws on the consideration of originality. The famous judgment by Peterson J on the distinction between "originality of ideas" and "expression of thought" was simple yet persuasive, which continues to be the reference of case decisions even for judges today.

However, one must bear in mind that copyright cases is a part of law which develops rapidly and will continue to provide much uncertainties when more and more forms of "literary works" are beginning to be made, such as AI generated text. I would encourage legal learners like myself to keep an open mind when reading past copyright judgments and look to the future simultaneously.

最后，彼得森法官考虑了被告的意见，即他们是根据“公平交易”规则，只是为了私人研究的目的而出版作品，这是该法明确允许的。根据事实，彼得森法官认为，由于相关作品已经由原告公司出版过一次，且被告公司没有添加足够的新颖信息以达到上述目的，因此判决被告公司侵犯了原告公司的著作权。

案件评述

本案仍然是关于考虑独创性的主要案例之一。彼得森法官关于“思想的独创性”和“想法的表达”之间区别的著名判决简单而有说服力，即使对今天的法官来说，它仍然是案件判决的参考。

然而，我们必须记住，版权案件是法律中发展迅速的一部分，当越来越多“文学作品”的形式开始出现时，它将继续产生许多不确定性，如人工智能生成的文本。像笔者一样的法律学习者，在阅读过去关于版权的判决的同时应保持开放的思想，展望未来。

Case 2 Coco v AN Clark (Engineers) Ltd
—How to keep a secret

Preface:

Information is traded everyday between individuals of distinct relationships; some are meant to be kept between the mouth that uttered it and the ears which heard it. There are secrets between friends, working partners, cooperations, and so on. In UK law of intellectual property, confidential information is well protected, and the persons whose secret was illegally used or communicated with a third party would enjoy the equitable rights to claim for breach of confidence. Due to an absence of statutory regulation, the judge in the present case had to devise an authoritative test.

Facts

The plaintiff designed a moped engine, the Coco moped, in 1965, to which he especially showcased his expertise on the design of the piston. By 1967 the first batch of the plaintiff's pistons were manufactured and the plaintiff, in the same year, approached the

案例2　可可诉 AN 克拉克（机械）有限公司案——如何保护秘密

引言：

各种信息每天都在不同关系的个人之间交换，有些则仅限于说出和听到的人之间。朋友之间、工作伙伴之间、合作伙伴之间等，都有秘密。在英国知识产权法中，保密信息得到了完善的保护，其秘密被非法使用或被交流给第三方的人将享有对其秘密被侵犯而进行索赔的衡平法权利。由于缺乏法律规定，本案的法官不得不设计一个权威的验证标准。

案件事实

原告于1965年设计了一台轻便摩托车发动机，可可摩托，该产品尤其展示了他在活塞设计方面的专业能力。至1967年，原告的第一批活塞已经被制造出来，同年，原告与被告公司接触，被告公司表示有兴趣签订制造发动机的协议。在接下来的

defendant company, who showed interest in forming an agreement to manufacture the engine. Over the next three months, the plaintiff and the defendant company worked closely together and the plaintiff provided the company with information, drawings and other form of resources to aid the company in the potential production of the moped engine. It is worth noting that there were never any contractual agreements signed or agreed between the parties.

On 20th July 1967, Mr Clark, the managing director of the defendant company made the plaintiff aware that he discovered a severe problem with the design of the moped, where the transmission was creating an unwanted amount of friction, in turn wearing the tyre. The defendant had also expressed to the plaintiff its intention to end the cooperation between the parties and design their own engine.

While the defendant company assured the plaintiff that their engine would not copy, or even be remotely similar to the Coco engine, the plaintiff nonetheless discovered later that the piston used in the defendant's engine design was almost identical to his design. The defendant later accepted that the piston used was in fact designed by the plaintiff, but they did not believe there were any elements of originality in the design.

The defendant company's engine subsequently went into production and was being sold, while the Coco engine had shown no signs of production. The plaintiff and Mr Mowbray, his representative claimed for the defendant company's misuse of private information which was given to the company in confidence,

3 个月里，原告和被告公司紧密合作，原告向被告公司提供了信息、图纸和其他各种形式的资源，以帮助被告公司形成生产轻便摩托车发动机的潜在可能。值得注意的是，双方之间从未签署或商定过任何合同协议。

1967 年 7 月 20 日，被告公司的常务董事克拉克先生告知原告，他发现轻便摩托车的设计存在严重问题，变速器产生了不必要的摩擦，从而磨损了轮胎。被告还向原告表示打算终止双方之间的合作，并自行设计发动机。

虽然被告公司向原告保证，他们的发动机不会仿效可可摩托，甚至与可可发动机相差甚远，但原告后来发现，被告发动机设计中使用的活塞与他的设计几乎相同。被告后来承认所使用的活塞实际上是由原告设计的，但他们不认为原告设计中有任何独创性。

被告公司的发动机随后投入生产并正在出售，而可可发动机则没有任何生产迹象。原告及其代理人莫伯雷先生就被告公司滥用原告提供的私有信息而提出索赔，原告提供的信息仅用于双方可能设立的合资企业，但此类信息现已用于被告公司自身的目的。他们寻求临时禁令的保护，以限制被告公司制造或

that the plaintiff supplied the information only for the purpose of a potential joint venture, yet such information has been utilized for the defendant company's own purpose. They sought an interlocutory injunction to limit the defendant company's ability to make or sell the engine.

Issue

Megarry J thought that there were two outstanding issues in need of consideration:

1. Whether there were in fact any breaches of the obligation of confidence?

2. Whether the injunction sought after by the plaintiff should be granted?

Judicial View

Breach of the obligation of confidence:

Megarry J expressed his doubts to the actual test that should be applied to cases such as the present one. He nonetheless argued that there should be three elements in deciding whether there existed a breach of confidence.

1. The information itself must "have the necessary quality of confidence about it";

2. That information must have been communicated in circumstances which would import and obligation of confidence;

销售发动机的能力。

争议焦点

梅加里法官认为有两个突出的问题需要考虑：

1. 在事实上是否违反保密义务？

2. 原告请求的临时禁令是否应当准予执行？

司法观点

违反保密义务：

梅加里法官对应适用于本案的实际测试表示怀疑。然而，他认为，在确定是否存在违反保密义务行为时，应当有三个要素。

1. 信息本身必须“具有保密的特质”；

2. 该信息必须是在存在保密义务的情形下传达的；

3. There must exist an unauthorised use of that information to the detriment of the communicating party.

— The information:

Megarry J cited a multiplicity of past case laws to aid him in the process of explaining the first element on the confidential nature of the information. He first quoted Lord Greene in the *Saltman* case, where he stated, *"something which is public property and public knowledge cannot per se provide any foundation for proceedings for breach of confidence."*[2] However, this sentence carries a degree of uncertainty, since "public property" is too narrow a concept. Something that was only constructed from materials in the public domain may still be confidential in nature, since the skill which was required to design or construct the said item originated from the ingenuity of the human brain. Megarry J argued, *"Novelty depends on the thing itself, and not upon the quality of its constituent parts."*

— The circumstances:

Megarry J asserted that to satisfy the circumstances element, the secret in question must not be communicated in public or in any circumstances that would negative or imply a non-performance for the duty of holding it confidential. Megarry J encountered much difficulty in this element, as there were no clear indications

[2] Saltman Engineering Co v Campbell Engineering Co Ltd, [1948] 65 RPC 203.

3. 必须存在未经授权使用该信息而损害披露方利益的情况。

——信息：

梅加里法官引用了许多过去的案例以帮助他解释有关信息保密性质的第一个要素。他首先引用了格林大法官在索尔特曼案中的话，他说，“**属于公共财产和公共知识的东西本身不能为违反保密的诉讼提供任何基础**”。[2]然而，这句话带有一定程度的不确定性，因为“公共财产”是一个过于狭隘的概念。一些仅由公共领域的材料制成的物品可能仍然是存在保密性的，因为设计或建造所述物品所需的技能源于人脑的独创性。梅加里法官认为，“**新颖性取决于事物本身，而不是其组成部分的特质**”。

——情形：

梅加里法官声称，如果想满足保密情形这一要素，该秘密不可以是公开传播的，也不得在任何可能否定或暗示不履行保密义务的情况下传播。梅加里法官在这一点上遇到了很多困难，因为过去的案例中，没有明确指出应采用哪些验证标准来支持保密情形这一论点。他最终决定使用合理性验证标准，

[2] 索尔特曼工程公司诉坎贝尔工程有限公司案，[1948] 65 RPC 203。

from past case laws on which tests should be applied to aid the circumstances argument. He ultimately decided to utilize the reasonableness test, where he argued,

"It seems to me that if the circumstances are such that any reasonable man standing in the shoes of the recipient of the information would have realised that upon reasonable grounds the information was being given to him in confidence, then this should suffice to impose upon him the equitable obligation of confidence."

Megarry J followed with an argument that especially in commercial situations is the duty likely to exist, or simply implied from the close partnership between the parties.

— The use and the detriment:

The third point was discussed briefly by Megarry J, where he was unsure whether there must have been detriment to the fulfilment of this element. Since the breach of confidence treads in the field of equity, Megarry J thought that detriment must have existed in some form or another, though this was still not absolute. Megarry J did not answer this question explicitly since there was obviously detriment suffered in the present case, he simply ended his analysis with, *"I need therefore say no more than that although for the purposes of this case I have stated the proposition in the stricter form, I wish to keep open the possibility of the true proposition being that in the wider form."*

认为，

在我看来，如果站在信息接收者的立场上的情形下，并且有理性的人会意识到，在合理的理由下，该信息是以保密方式给予他的，则这应足以使他承担衡平法中的保密义务。

梅加里法官接着提出了一个论点，即特别是在商业情形下该义务很可能存在，或双方之间密切伙伴关系中即简单地隐含有该义务。

——使用及损害：

梅加里法官简要地讨论了第三点，他不确定这一要素的满足是否必须存在损害后果。由于保密义务的违反涉及了衡平法的领域，梅加里法官认为，损害必须以某种形式存在，但是这仍然不是绝对的。梅加里没有明确回答这个问题，因为在本案出现了对原告明显的损害后果，他只是说："因此，我只需要说，尽管为了本案的目的，我已经以较为严格的形式陈述了这一观点，但我希望真实观点以更广泛形式存在的可能性得以保留。"

Application of each element to the current case

— Circumstance:

Megarry J started his analysis on the second element of circumstance since he thought, upon the facts, this element was the most obvious. He argued that in many cases where the agreement of confidentiality was not expressed stated, we must rely on the implied intentions between the parties. Megarry J used an example to clarify the potential situation, *"Do you not think that you ought to have an express agreement that everything you are discussing is confidential? I think the parties would have testily suppressed him with a common 'But it obviously is'"*. Therefore, Megarry J decided that the correct test to apply for the second element is that, whether the two parties had formed an express agreement on confidentiality, and if they did not, whether their answer would be along the lines of "obviously" when asked about the confidentiality of the information being communicated. Megarry J was satisfied that according to the facts of the current case, there were implied confidentiality between the plaintiff and Mr Clark's company on the design of the moped engine, at least in equity, where both parties would be asked to abide by good conscience, instead of stringent duties of law.

— Confidentiality of the information and the use:

Megarry J combined his analysis on the first and third elements of the test. He first stated that due to a lack of information and

各要素在本案中的适用

——情形：

梅加里法官首先适用了第二个因素，保密情形，因为他认为在本案的事实上，这个因素是最明显的。他认为，在那些诸多的没有明示保密协议的情况下，我们必须依赖当事人之间的默示意图。梅加里法官举了一个例子来阐明可能发生的情况，“你们不认为你们应该有明确的协议以约定你们所讨论的一切都是保密的吗？我认为两方会用一个普通的‘但我们显然是啊’来回答”。因此，梅加里法官决定，适用第二个要素的正确验证标准是，双方是否就保密问题达成了明确协议，如果没有，当被问及所传达信息的保密性时，他们的回答是否符合“显然”的意思。梅加里法官确信，根据本案的事实，原告和克拉克先生的公司之间对轻便摩托车发动机的设计有默示的保密，至少在衡平法上是这样，双方均被要求遵守良心，而不是严格的法律义务。

——信息的保密及使用：

梅加里法官结合了他对测试的第一和第三要素的分析。他首先认为，由于缺乏资料和对证据的交叉询问，他对原告的设

cross-examination of the evidence, he remained in darkness as to the availability of the plaintiff's design in the open market. Though the defendant argued that the parts which they purchased that were similar to the plaintiff's design were easily attainable on the market. What then was left for the courts to decide was, how far the defendant's product "*achieves these similarities by drawing on confidential information imparted by the plaintiff in confidence*" and whether the Coco engine was produced with originality and information which may suggest confidentiality. Upon analysing the specific facts, where was omitted in the decision, the court held that the plaintiff had not produced enough or compelling evidence to point towards the confidential nature of the information, and the relevant evidence had failed to reveal that the similarities between the engines were the result of illegal usage of the plaintiff's design.

Megarry J also considered the plaintiff's claim for interlocutory injunction, which was based on another case, *Terrapin*, where the court thought that the two defendants had illegally obtained information from the plaintiff during their 5 years collaboration, and such evidence necessitated an interlocutory injunction. Megarry J argued that while the plaintiff made a strong argument referencing the *Terrapin* case, there were material differences between Terrapin and the present case. First, the present case lacks cross-examination on the evidence to produce significant factors for consideration. Second, the plaintiff in the present case implied that there were elements of fraud on the part of the defendant, such allegations did not appear in *Terrapin*. Third, both the plaintiff and the defendant in

计在公开市场上是否存在一无所知。但是被告辩称，他们购买的与原告设计相似的零件在市场上很容易获得。所以现在留给法院裁定的是，“**被告的产品在多大程度上通过利用原告秘密提供的机密信息来实现这些相似性**”，以及可可设计的引擎是否存在独创性和保密性。在对判决中省略了的具体事实进行分析后，法院认为，原告没有提供足够或令人信服的证据来证明信息的机密性，而相关证据也未能揭示发动机之间的相似性是被告非法使用原告设计的结果。

梅加里法官还考虑了原告的临时禁令请求，该请求基于另一个案件，即特若平（Terrapin）公司案，其中法院认为，两个被告公司在与原告进行5年的合作期间非法从原告处获得了信息，这样的证据足够触发临时禁令。梅加里法官认为，虽然本案中原告引用特若平公司案提出了强有力的论点，但特若平公司案与本案之间存在实质性差异。第一，本案缺乏对证据的交叉询问，继而未产生重要的考量因素。第二，本案中的原告暗示，被告方面存在欺诈的要素，此类指控并未出现在特若平公司案中。第三，特若平公司案中的原告和被告的相关产品均已投入生产，而本案中只有被告公司投入生产。

Terrapin went into production for their relevant products, while in the present case only the defendant company went into production.

Comments

Ultimately, the court dismissed the claim for breach of obligation of confidentiality and rejected the request of an interlocutory injunction. However, the significance of this case lies in Megarry J's clarification on the three-part test of confidentiality and has since been in use through most breach of confidentiality cases in the UK.

Confidential information is just as important to individuals as they are to corporates. It is a pleasant sight that the English courts are taking such tremendous efforts to ensure the protection of such information.

案件评述

法院最终驳回了关于违反保密义务的指控，并驳回了临时禁令的请求。然而，本案的意义在于梅加里法官对保密性三部分验证标准的澄清，并且该验证标准在英国大多数违反保密义务的案件中被广泛使用。

机密信息对个人来说和其对公司一样重要。令人欣慰的是，英国法院正在付出巨大的努力来确保对这些信息的保护。

Case 3 Kogan v Martin

—How to be recognized as a joint author of a copyrighted work

Preface:

It is never truly enough to depend on one person for the creation of great projects, individuals come together and collaborate for all kinds of literary, dramatic and artistic works. It is then left for law to ensure that no one's contribution goes unnoticed, while trivial and minimal efforts do not unjustly or unlawfully affect the intellectual creations of another. The law on Joint Authorship serves this very purpose, though the courts have always been puzzled as to the extent of what one needs to contribute in order to be considered as a joint author. This relatively recent landmark case from the UK Court of Appeal may offer guidance as the judges concerned identified a new test for joint authorship.

Facts

The appellant, Ms Kogan was and is a professional opera

案例 3　科根诉马丁案
——如何被认定为版权作品的共同作者

引言：

仅仅依靠一个人来创造伟大的项目是远远不够的，人们经常聚集在一起，合作完成各种文学、戏剧和艺术作品。法律需要确保任何人的贡献均不会被忽视，同时，一些微不足道的努力也不可不公正或非法地影响属于他人的智力创造。关于共同作者的法律正是为这一目的服务的，但是法院一直对一个人需要贡献什么才能被视为共同作者的问题感到困惑。来自英国上诉法院的这一相对较新的里程碑式案例可能对此提供指导，因为相关法官确立了一个新的共同作者标准。

案件事实

上诉人科根女士迄今是一名专业歌剧演唱家，但她一直对

singer, but she had always had passion towards writing, to which she authored three children's books in her twenties and had also created her own theatre projects. The respondent, Mr Martin was and is a professional writer, who had contributed and authored 12 short films, 3 plays and 9 feature films. The two individuals met during late 2011 and soon got into a romantic relationship. Despite both being fascinated by each other's professions, their relationship came to an end in 2014.

The dispute revolves around a script for the film "Florence Foster Jenkins" (FFJ), which is centred around a woman of that name who was a famous singer. The relevant facts on the script are as follows:

Ms Kogan stated in her witness statement that she had first heard about FFJ in 1991 and had since been interested in this individual. Ms Kogan stated that she showed Mr Martin video clips of FFJ singing and had communicated to him the idea of a film script based on her. Mr Martin rejected this statement and insisted that he discovered Ms Kogan listening to FFJ and formed the idea by himself of writing a film script on her after several days of research.

The first draft of the screenplay ("the Florence project") was finished by April 2013 and the second one was completed by June in the same year. Before the final version's completion, the two had broken up and were no longer in a relationship. By 2016, the screenplay was used for the release of the film "Florence Foster Jenkins". Mr Martin sought a declaration that he was the sole author

写作充满激情，她在 20 多岁时创作了 3 本儿童读物，并创作了自己的戏剧项目。被告马丁先生一直是一名专业作家，曾创作了 12 部短片、3 部戏剧和 9 部故事片。两人在 2011 年年末相遇，并且很快就确定了情侣关系。尽管两人都对对方的职业着迷，但他们的关系在 2014 年结束。

本案争议围绕着电影《弗洛伦斯 · 福斯特 · 詹金斯（跑调天后）》（FFJ）的剧本展开，该剧本是关于片名女子，一位著名歌手。剧本草稿的相关事实如下：

科根女士在她的证人陈述中说，她第一次听到弗洛伦斯 · 福斯特 · 詹金斯是 1991 年，且此后一直对这个人感兴趣。科根女士表示，她向马丁先生展示了弗洛伦斯 · 福斯特 · 詹金斯唱歌的视频片段，并向他交流了以她为原型创作电影剧本的想法。马丁先生否定了该说法，坚持认为他当时发现了科根女士在听弗洛伦斯 · 福斯特 · 詹金斯女士的歌曲，并在经过几天的研究后自己形成了为她写电影剧本的想法。

剧本初稿（“弗洛伦斯项目”）于 2013 年 4 月完成，第二稿于同年 6 月完成。在最终版本完成之前，两人已经分手且不再有关系。2016 年，使用该剧本的电影《弗洛伦斯 · 福斯特 · 詹金斯（跑调天后）》上映。马丁先生要求声明他是该剧本的唯一作者，而科根女士则提起反诉要求宣布她为共同作者。

of the screenplay and Ms Kogan sought after a counterclaim to declare her as the joint author.

During the proceedings Mr Martin accepted the following facts:

— Ms Kogan provided information on music, especially the lifestyle, vocabulary, and idioms of opera singers.

— Ms Kogan criticised and provided feedback on drafts of the screenplay.

— Ms Kogan contributed to observations made on FFJ and her interests in music.

— Ms Kogan's suggestions occasionally contributed to lines of dialogue, on very few occasions included in the script.

— Ms Kogan suggested several creative ideas for minor characters and events in the script.

More details are here omitted for the purpose of simplicity and to avoid unnecessary complexity.

Issue

Under which standards and circumstances can a copyrighted work be seen in law as the work of joint authorship?

Judicial View

The law:

Section 10 (1) of the Copyright, Designs and Patents Act 1988

诉讼过程中，马丁先生认可了以下事实：

—— 科根女士提供了有关音乐的信息，特别是歌剧演员的生活方式、词汇和习语。

—— 科根女士对剧本草稿提出了批评并提供了反馈。

—— 科根女士对弗洛伦斯·福斯特·詹金斯的观察和她对音乐的兴趣做出了贡献。

—— 科根女士的建议偶尔会有助于对白的内容，但在剧本中很少出现。

—— 科根女士为剧本中的次要人物和事件提出了一些具有创造性的想法。

为了简单性和避免不必要的复杂性，这里省略了诸多细节。

争议焦点

在什么标准和情况下，一个版权作品在法律上可以被视为共同创作的作品？

司法观点

法律条文：

《1988 年版权、设计和专利法》（本文中简称该法）第 10

("the Act") provides:

"(1) In this Part a 'work of joint authorship' means a work produced by the collaboration of two or more authors in which the contribution of each author is not distinct from that of the other author or authors."

First instance court:

The Intellectual Property Enterprise Court (IPEC), after viewing all the relevant facts declared that Mr Martin was, in law the sole author of the screenplay and the sole owner of the copyright. The judge approached the case in a factual manner, where he did not believe there to be enough relevant input from Ms Kogan, that *"Ms Kogan's textual and non-textual contributions never rose above the level of providing useful jargon, along with helpful criticism and some minor plot suggestions."*

Ms Kogan appealed against this decision and the matter reached the Court of Appeal.

The Court of Appeal decision:

Floyd LJ separated the requirements in section 10 of the Act to four main parts, an intelligent approach which remains as the authoritative test for joint authorship cases: a) Collaboration, b) Authorship, c) Contribution, and d) Non-distinctiveness of contribution.

（1）条规定：

（1）在本部分，“合著作品”是指由两名或多于两名作者合作创作的作品，而其中每名作者的贡献与另一名或多于一名作者的贡献并无分别。

一审法院判决：

知识产权企业法院（IPEC）在查看所有相关事实后判定，马丁先生在法律上是该剧本的唯一作者和版权的所有者。法官以实事求是的方式处理案件，认为科根女士没有提供足够的相关贡献，“科根女士的文本和非文本贡献从未超过提供有用行话、有用的评价和一些小情节建议的层次”。

科根女士对这一决定提出上诉，该事项被提交至上诉法院。

上诉法院判决：

弗洛伊德大法官将该法第10条的要求分为四个主要部分，这是一种非常睿智的方法，且仍然是对共同作者案例的权威验证标准：a）合作；b）作者身份；c）贡献；d）贡献的不区分性。

a) Collaboration:

Floyd LJ began his analysis on collaboration with a quote from Keating J in Beckingham v Hodgens [2003] EWCA Civ 143, *"Each would be contributing to the whole production, and they might be said to be joint authors of it. But, to constitute joint authorship, there must be a common design."*

Floyd LJ focused on the nature of the collaboration, that the authors must both clearly intend to work together for the purpose of the completion of the work, but not mere suggestions or criticisms by friends or colleagues. It was in Floyd LJ's opinion that the quantity of contribution is not the most important factor. He used an example of a person adding significant contribution as a friend's advice, but the friend's version of the literary work becomes widely known and the corrections he made were extensive and material, this would nonetheless be considered the work of a sole author since neither of the parties considered it a work of joint authorship. This was contrasted with the case of *Beckingham v Hodgens*, where a mere contribution of a four-bar riff to a pop song was considered the work of a joint authorship since there were clear evidences pointing towards collaborative efforts. Floyd LJ emphasized on the importance of identifying the true nature of the interaction between the individuals during the creation of the work. He also specifically mentioned that in a literary work, a person can be considered a joint author even if he or she did not contribute at all to the writing but instead towards the idea and the creative process.

a）合作：

弗洛伊德大法官引用了基廷法官在贝金汉诉霍金斯案（[2003]EWCA Civ 143）中的一句话，并开始了他对合作的分析，“每个人都会对整个作品作出贡献，可以说他们是作品的共同作者。但是，要构成共同作者，必须有一个共同的设计”。

弗洛伊德大法官重点讨论了合作的性质，即作者们必须明确打算为了完成作品而共同努力，而不仅仅是朋友或同事的建议或评价。弗洛伊德大法官认为贡献的数量不是最重要的因素。他举了一个例子，一个人作为朋友，在提出建议时增加了重要的贡献，但他的作品版本变得广为人知，他所作的更正广泛而重要，但这将被视为单一作者的作品，因双方均不认为它是共同作者的作品。这与贝金汉诉霍金斯案形成了对比，在该案中，对一首流行歌曲的四小节即兴的贡献被认定为共同作者的作品，因为有明确证据表明了合作付出的努力。弗洛伊德大法官强调了在作品创作过程中确定个人之间互动的真实本质的重要性。

他还特别提到，在文学作品中，一个人即使没有对写作做出任何贡献，也可以通过对思想和创作过程做出的贡献而成为共同作者。

b) Authorship:

Floyd LJ cited section 9 (1) of the Act to begin his view on authorship, where it stated the author is *"the person who creates it."* He declared that a work of joint authorship is *"a work produced by the collaboration of all the persons who created that work."*

Floyd LJ again referenced case law to aid his analysis, where Laddie J stated in *Cala Homes [1995] F.S.R. 818* that *"In my view, to have regard merely to who pushed the pen is too narrow a view of authorship."* Floyd J wished to use this statement to communicate the core idea that authorship is not confined to the person who puts the ideas down to the paper, but rather *"the skill and effort involved in creating, selecting or gather together the detailed concepts or emotions which the words have fixed in writing."*

c) Contribution:

Contribution, as Floyd LJ put it, must be an "authorial" one. The diction on "authorial" is not fixed, but varies from work to work. For instance, a person who fixes bugs of a computer software cannot be said to be a joint author since his contribution does not lie within the creation process, in turn not qualifying as "authorial". Floyd LJ argued that for screenplays such as the one in the present case, what counts as an authorial contribution should have the power to make the reader visualize what might happen on the screen and contribute towards the overall feeling of the audience.

Another question was how much contribution must be made for a

b）作者身份：

弗洛伊德大法官引用了该法第 9（1）条，开始阐述他对作者身份的看法，其中指出作者是“创造它的人”。他明示，共同作者的作品是“由所有创作该作品的人共同创作的作品”。

弗洛伊德大法官再次引用了案例来辅助他的分析，兰迪法官在卡拉霍姆案（[1995] F.S.R.818）中指出，“在我看来，仅仅考虑谁推动了写作而界定作者身份的看法太狭隘了”。弗洛伊德大法官希望利用该陈述表达这样一个核心观点，即作者身份不仅限于将想法写在纸上的人，而是“创造、选择或收集固化在文字中的详细概念或情感的技巧和努力”。

c）贡献：

正如弗洛伊德大法官所说，贡献必须是“作家的”。“作家的”这一措辞不是固定不变的，而是因作品而异。例如，修复计算机软件缺陷的人不能说是共同作者，因为他的贡献不在创作过程中，反过来也不符合“作家的”资格。弗洛伊德大法官认为，如本案中的剧本，作者的贡献应该具备让读者想象屏幕上可能发生的事情的力量，且有助于观众的整体感觉。

另一个问题是，一个撰稿人要成为共同作者，须做出多少

contributor to become a joint author. Floyd LJ chose to adapt a renowned EU law term, which was first mentioned in the famous *Infopaq* case[3]: The author's own intellectual creation. This simple term has now become the authority on all EU copyright cases concerning authorship. The essence of the term is that the author must have demonstrated extensive and creative choices and skill in producing the work.

d) The non-distinctiveness of the contribution:

The final element requires the efforts of the authors to be a unitary whole, and not separated. This element explains itself since there should not be a discussion for joint authorship if the efforts made by the parties are so distinct, that they form different paths and works.

Hacon J's theories and Floyd LJ's criticism:

Another point of great significance is Floyd LJ's criticism and abolishment on Hacon J's theories in the first instance court.

Hacon J suggested two tests, namely the ultimate arbiter test and the primary/secondary skills test:

The ultimate arbiter:

Hacon J addressed the fact that Ms Kogan accepted that Mr

[3] Infopag International A/S v Danske Dagblades Forening (C-5/08) [2012] Bus. L. R. 102.

贡献。弗洛伊德大法官选择了一个著名的欧盟法律术语，该术语首先在著名的因弗派克案[3]中被提及：作者自己的智力创造。这个简单的术语现在已经成为所有涉及作者身份的欧盟版权案件的权威。该术语的实质是，作者必须在创作作品时表现出广泛和创造性的选择和技巧。

d）贡献的不区分性：

最后一个要素要求作者们的努力是一个统一的整体，而不是分开的。这一要素顾名思义，因为如果当事方所作的努力如此不同，以至于它们形成不同的路径和作品，就不应讨论共同作者的问题。

哈孔法官的理论与弗洛伊德洛大法官对此的批评：

本案另一个重要意义，是弗洛伊德大法官对哈孔法官在一审中提出的理论的批判和废除。

哈孔法官建议考虑两项验证标准，即最终裁决者验证标准和主要 / 次要技能验证标准：

最终裁决者：

哈孔法官指出，科根女士承认马丁先生有权决定剧本的最终版本及其内容，并称他为“最终裁决者”，这是使他最初被

[3] 因弗派克国际股份公司诉丹麦报业协会案，(C-5/08)[2012]Bus. L. R. 102。

Martin had the power to decide the final version of the script and its contents, naming him as the "ultimate arbiter", that this was one of the more vital factors to his initial recognition as the sole author. Hacon J stated that while the ultimate arbiter test could be relevant in future cases, it cannot be determinative. Floyd LJ thought that Hacon J produced insufficient consideration for this test, that it was uncertain whether Hacon J meant for this test to be applied to the element of collaboration, or any other elements.

The distinction between primary / secondary skills:

Hacon J argued that there should exist a distinction between the primary and secondary skills operated by the author. He inferred that in copyright cases primary skills, such as the use of a pencil, brush or other means to create images should be given more weight when considering authorship. Secondary skills are for instance the selection of scenes in a screenplay, or the selection of colour in a painting, those skills are to be given less weight, meaning for an individual to be considered a joint author, it would be easier for him or her to do so had they contributed primary skills as opposed to secondary ones. Floyd LJ thought that it was, to a great extend incorrect to create a distinction in law between primary and secondary skills, that secondary skills are to be seen as equals when considering contributions. Floyd LJ further argued that such distinctions have no basis either in statutes or case laws, and such distinction adds more uncertainty to the law of joint authorship.

承认为唯一作者的更重要的因素之一。哈孔法官说，虽然最终裁决者验证标准在今后的案件中可能存在相关性，但它不能是决定性的。弗洛伊德大法官认为，哈孔法官对该验证标准的考虑不足，不确定哈孔法官是否打算将该验证标准应用于合作元素或任何其他元素。

主要和次要技能之间的区别：

哈孔法官认为，作者操作的主要技能和次要技能之间应有分别。他推断，在版权案件的主要技能，如使用铅笔、画笔或其他手段来创建图像时，应在考虑作者身份时给予更多的分量。次要技能如剧本中的场景选择或绘画中的色彩选择，这些技能的权重较小，意味着对个人来说，如果他们贡献了主要技能而不是次要技能，那么他或她将更容易被视为共同作者。弗洛伊德大法官认为，在法律上区分主要和次要技能在很大程度上是不正确的，在考虑贡献时，次要技能应被视为与主要技能平等。弗洛伊德大法官进一步认为，这种区分在成文法或案例法中均无依据，并且给共同作者的法律增加了更多的不确定性。

The court then spent an overwhelming amount of time on the analysis of specific contributions and facts in the case, which would here be omitted. The court held that the efforts made by Ms Kogan satisfied the four-part test and that in the end the appeal by Ms Kogan was allowed and the first instance judges' declaration was to be set aside. A new trial was ordered to be commenced before a different judge in the IPEC.

Comments

Certain joint authorship cases can be unfortunate, to see two individuals once in love to now sit at the opposite sides of a cold legal dispute, it is nonetheless vital for the law of copyright to ensure that real efforts do not go unprotected. The significance of this case lies in the orderly judgment by Floyd LJ, where he considered each element of joint authorship in turn and rejected previous authoritative tests. The overall position towards joint authorship now becomes less narrow, and more accepting of different contributions made by different individuals.

法院花了大量时间分析本案的具体贡献和事实，此处省略。法院认为，科根女士的努力满足了四个部分的标准，最终她的上诉被支持，一审法官的判决被撤销。裁定知识产权企业法院指派另一名法官重新审理本案。

案件评述

某些共同作者案件是不幸的，看到两个曾经相爱的人现在坐在冰冷的法律纠纷的对立面，尽管如此，确保真正的努力得到保护在版权法中是至关重要的。本案的意义在于弗洛伊德大法官有序的判决，他依次考虑了共同作者的每个要素，并拒绝了先前的权威验证标准。现在，共同作者的总体立场变得不那么狭隘，且更多地接受了不同个体的不同贡献。

Part Three: Selected Cases under Anti-discrimination Law

第三部分：反歧视法案例

Case 1 A Institution v Ahmed

—Separation between "intention" and "ground" in Anti-discrimination law

Preface:

More and more cases of inequality of treatment based on a person's specific characteristics arise each year, both inside and outside of employment. Racism and sexism are two growing concerns of discriminations that are under the spotlight especially in western countries. The last decade has been crucial for the law makers in the United Kingdom, as judges and the parliament put in great efforts to decrease the tendencies of discrimination in the UK. Nevertheless, such acts are easier said than done, discriminations come in many forms and the discriminator carries varied intentions, some more malicious than others, some may even be done in good faith. This article will outline the basics of direct discrimination law in the UK and the role of intention in judges' considerations through a major case law and a few statutory explanations.

案例 1　A 机构诉艾哈迈德案
——反歧视法中“意图”与“理由”的分割

引言：

无论是在工作环境之内还是之外，每年都有越来越多的基于个人具体特征的不平等待遇案件出现。特别是在西方国家，种族歧视和性别歧视是两个日益受到关注的问题。过去 10 年对英国的立法者至关重要，其间，法官和议会均做出了巨大努力以减少英国歧视事件的发生频率。然而，这说来容易做起来难，歧视有多种形式，并且歧视者的意图多种多样，有些出于恶意，有些甚至可能是出于善意。本文将通过一个主要的案例和一些成文法条，概述英国反歧视法中直接歧视的基本内容以及歧视者意图在法官考虑中的作用。

Facts

The claimant Ahmed, who is of north Sudanese origin was refused promotion by her employer A Institution for the position of researcher in Sudan. The employer argued that it refused Ahmed for her own safety considerations and with positive intentions. Ahmed being from the north with an "Arab" appearance may invoke conflicts due to the political tensions happening in Sudan between the south and the north. Ahmed and her team may be the target of violence in the local area, which is why A Institution has prohibited all employees from working in their "own" nations. The claimant has since resigned and claimed for direct discrimination by A Institution.

Issue

1. What are the mandatory requirements for Direct discrimination?

2. What is the role of "ground" and "intention" in Anti-discrimination law? And What is their difference?

Judicial View

Direct discrimination:

Before reading the judge's arguments on the present case, one must understand the basics of direct discrimination in the UK.

案件事实

申请人艾哈迈德是北苏丹裔，她的雇主A机构拒绝了她在苏丹的研究员职位。雇主辩称，拒绝艾哈迈德是出于对她自身安全考虑以及正面的意图。由于苏丹南部和北部之间的政治紧张局势，艾哈迈德具有的北方“阿拉伯”容貌可能在当地引发冲突。艾哈迈德和她的团队可能成为当地暴力行为的目标，这就是A机构禁止所有雇员在自己国家工作的原因。申请人后来辞职，并起诉A机构实施了直接歧视。

争议焦点

1. 直接歧视有哪些强制性规定？

2. “理由”和“意图”在反歧视法中的作用是什么？它们的区别是什么？

司法观点

直接歧视：

在阅读法官对本案的论点之前，我们必须了解直接歧视在英国的基础概念。《1976年种族关系法》将直接歧视定义为：

Direct discrimination was defined in the Race Relations Act 1976 as:

"A person discriminates against another in any circumstances relevant for the purposes of any provision of this Act if (a) on racial grounds he treats that other less favourably than he treats or would treat other persons ..."

The main focus in this definition is on "less favourably", "other persons" and "racial grounds."

Less favourably: this requires the treatment to carry with it some sort of detriment onto the claimant, mere different treatments will not suffice.

Other persons: there exists the need of a comparator, hypothetical or not, to be under similar circumstances with the claimant and possess with him/her the opposite protected characteristic. For instance, the comparator of a discriminated person of African origins in the workplace should be a Caucasian employee in the same position.

Racial grounds: the source of the less favourable treatment which the claimant had received must have originated or based off his/her race.

The first instance court:

The case was first decided by the Employment Tribunal (ET), where it found that direct discrimination existed and A Institution acted in contrary to the Race Relations Act 1976, since it was clear that the denial of the claimant's promotion was racially motivated.

任何人在与本法任何规定有关的任何情况下对另一人构成歧视，如果（a）基于种族原因，他对待另一人劣于他对待或将要对待其他人……

这一定义的主要重点是“劣于”“其他人”“种族理由”。

劣于：该点要求申请人受到的待遇为其带来某种损害，仅仅不同的待遇不够达到此条件。

其他人：需找到一名比较者。无论是否是假设的，比较者都有必要与申请人处于类似的情况，并与申请人具有相反的受保护特征。例如，非洲裔受歧视者在工作场所的比较对象应是同一职位的白人雇员。

种族理由：申请人所获得的劣于待遇必须源于或基于其种族。

一审法院：

该案首先由就业法庭（ET）裁定，该法庭认定存在直接歧视，A 机构的行为违反了《1976 年种族关系法》，因为他们拒绝申请人的晋升显然是出于种族动机。A 机构针对该决定向就业上诉法庭（EAT）提出上诉。

A Institution appealed against this decision to the Employment Appeal Tribunal (EAT).

The Employment Appeal Tribunal:

Underhill J began his analysis on direct discrimination with the opinions and judgment by the first instance court and the respondent's arguments against the previous judgment. There were two grounds which the respondent relied on in their appeal to state that the employment tribunal had erred in its judgment:

1. that the hypothetical comparator the tribunal constructed was not appropriate and in fact incorrect.

2. that the tribunal failed to take into consideration the "reasons" behind why Amnesty rejected the claimant of her promotion.

The hypothetical comparator argument:

Underhill J first cited the judgment by the ET on the construction of the hypothetical comparator, *"In our judgment the hypothetical comparator here is any similarly or identically qualified applicant as the claimant, with the same level of experience, who was of non-Sudanese ethnicity."* While Underhill J did not expressly state whether the ET erred in its construction, he did state that, *"consideration of what should be the characteristic of a hypothetical comparator is often a less useful way of addressing the questions raised by an issue of direct discrimination than focusing on the fundamental question of the reason for the act*

就业上诉法庭：

昂德希尔法官从一审法院的意见和判决以及被申请人反对先前判决的论点开始分析直接歧视。被申请人在上诉中提出两个理由，称就业法庭的判决有误：

1. 法庭所假设的比较者是不适当的，事实上是不正确的。

2. 法庭没有考虑到A机构拒绝申请人晋升的背后的“理由”。

假设比较者论点：

昂德希尔法官首先引用了就业法庭关于假设比较者构造的判决，“在我们的判决中，假设的比较者是任何与申请人具有类似或相同资格的申请者，并具有相同的经验水平，且属于非苏丹族裔”。虽然昂德希尔法官没有明确说明就业法庭的构造是否有错误，但他指出：“在处理关于直接歧视的问题时，考虑一个假设的比较者应该具有什么样的特征，往往不如把重点放在所起诉行为的理由这一基本问题上。”因此，本案讨论的主要焦点是，法院是否应考虑到申请人得到劣于待遇的“原因”。

complained of." Therefore, the primary focus of discussion was on whether the court should take into consideration the "reason why" the claimant received less favourable treatment.

The intention argument:

The intention argument focuses on the "grounds" of discrimination, to put it plainly, what was the reason behind the claimant's denial of promotion? The respondent attempted to argue that the ET only considered one of the two factors required to fulfil the "grounds" requirement. Mr Epstein, who represented the respondent stated that the first factor was to ask whether "but for" the claimant's race, she was denied promotion and the second factor being the "intention" behind the denial of promotion. Mr Epstein further argued that the ET only considered the first factor, but neglected the second factor.

The main question which was placed before the Employment Appeal Tribunal and primarily before Underhill J, was the distinction between the objective "grounds", or "reasons" of less favourable treatment and the subjective "intention" and "motivation" inside the respondent's mind. To make it easier to understand, the objective "grounds" could be that the employer did not believe the employee was qualified for the job, regardless of the employee's ethnicity, yet the employee so happened to be Sudanese. The subjective "intention" could be that the employer knew that promoting a northern Sudanese employee may carry risks of violence and physical safety of the employee. In both situations

意图论点：

意图论点集中于歧视的“理由”，简单地说，申请人被拒绝晋升的原因是什么？被申请人试图主张就业法庭只考虑了满足“理由”要求所需的两个因素之一。代表被申请人的爱泼斯坦先生说，第一个因素是询问是否“若非”申请人的种族而使她被拒绝晋升，第二个因素是拒绝晋升背后的“意图”。爱泼斯坦先生进一步认为法庭只考虑了第一个因素，而忽略了第二个因素。

就业上诉法庭和昂德希尔法官面临的主要问题是，劣于待遇的客观“理由”或“原因”与被申请人内心的主观“意图”和“动机”之间的区别。为了更容易理解，客观“理由”可以是雇主不相信雇员有资格胜任这项工作且与雇员的种族无关，但雇员恰好是苏丹人。主观“意图”可能是雇主知道提拔北苏丹雇员可能会带来暴力和雇员人身安全的风险。在这两种情况下，雇主均不能被视为“种族主义者”，但昂德希尔法官认为这两种客观和主观原因是完全不同的。

the employer cannot be considered "racist", yet Underhill J believed the two objective and subjective reasons are completely different.

Before starting the analysis on the difference between the two reasons, one must be familiar with the two dominant cases which the respondent attempted to use to argue that the ET erred in law. The respondent argued that there exists a problematic conflict between the reasoning in the two cases below.

James v Eastleigh Borough Council, [1990] ICR 554:

The plaintiff in James, 61 years old, was charged for swimming pool service when attempting to enter the facility with his wife of the same age. His wife was not charged since the swimming pool allowed free entry for pensioners and the pensionable age for woman was 60, while it was 65 for men. The Council as the respondent which charged the plaintiff tried to argue that they were merely following the pension scheme and had no intention to discriminate against men, that the "purpose" was not to ensure men would receive less favourable treatments. Lord Goff in James utilized the renowned "but for" test and submitted that, *"Would the plaintiff, a man of 61, have received the same treatment as his wife but for his sex? An affirmative answer is inescapable."* The Council was ultimately found to be discriminatory.

The ET in the present case used James to rule against A Institution in the first instance by stating that "but for" the claimant's race, she would not be denied promotion.

While Mr Epstein and the respondent recognized the binding

在分析这两个原因之间的差异之前，必须熟悉被申请人为了论证就业法庭在法律上的错误而试图利用的两个主要案例。被申请人指称，以下两个案件的推理之间存在复杂的冲突。

詹姆斯诉伊斯特利行政区委员会案，［1990］ICR 554：

詹姆斯案的申请人当时61岁，在试图与其同龄妻子进入游泳设施时被要求为游泳池的使用而付费。由于游泳池允许退休人员免费进入，女性的退休年龄为60岁，而男性为65岁，因此他的妻子没有被收取任何费用。被申请人委员会试图辩称，他们只是在遵循退休计划，无意歧视男性，他们的“目的”不是为了确保男性获得劣于待遇。詹姆斯案中的戈夫大法官使用了著名的“若非”验证标准，并提出“**若非因为申请人不同的性别，61岁的他会和他的妻子受到同样的待遇吗？答案是肯定的**”，该委员会最终被认为构成歧视。

本案中，就业法庭在一审中利用詹姆斯案对A机构裁决，称“若非”申请人的种族，她不会被拒绝晋升。

虽然爱泼斯坦先生和被申请人承认詹姆斯案具有约束力，

power of James, they centred their appeal around another significant case, which may have argued that the "intention" of the less favourable treatment must also be relevant, the respondent believed that the reasoning in the case conflict with the "but for" test in James.

Nagarajan v London Regional Transport, [1999] ICR 877:

The applicant claimed to be denied appointment to a job due to his previous race discrimination claims against it or associated companies. The tribunal at the time upheld his claim and found that the decision-makers were "consciously or subconsciously" influenced by the knowledge of his previous complaints. When this case reached the House of Lords, Lord Nicholls stated, *"Save in obvious cases, answering the crucial question will call for some consideration of the mental processes of the alleged discriminator."*

Mr Epstein and the respondent in the present case wished to argue that this statement by Lord Nicholls constructed the requirement that the mental processes of the alleged discriminator must be relevant.

With the two cases at hand, Underhill J discovered a key difference between the two scenarios in the cases. In James, the act in itself is discriminatory, the treatment complained of is inherent in the act itself, the entry to the swimming pool was, as Lord Goff put it, "gender-based". Underhill J submitted that, in cases such as James when the act itself contains discriminatory treatments, the intentions and motive of the discriminator becomes irrelevant since

但他们在上诉中的辩论集中于另一个重要案件，该案件可能提出劣于待遇的“意图”也必须是相关的，被申请人认为该案件中的理由与詹姆斯案中的“若非”验证标准相冲突。

纳加拉贾诉伦敦地区交通局案，[1999] ICR 877：

申请人声称由于他以前对伦敦地区交通局或其相关公司的种族歧视指控而被其拒绝给予工作。法庭当时支持他的申诉，认为决策者“有意识或无意识地”受到他先前对其指控的影响。当这个案件到达上议院时，尼科尔斯大法官说道：“除了明显的案件外，回答这个关键问题需要对涉案歧视者的心理过程进行一些考虑。”

爱泼斯坦先生和本案的被申请人意图辩称，尼科尔斯大法官的这一陈述构成了一项要求，即涉案歧视者的心理过程必须是相关的。

有了这两个案例，昂德希尔法官发现了案例中两个场景之间的关键区别。在詹姆斯案中，这一行为本身就是歧视性的，所申诉的劣于待遇是该行为本身固有，进入游泳池，正如戈夫大法官所说，是“基于性别”的。昂德希尔法官认为，在诸如詹姆斯这样的案件中，当行为本身包含歧视性待遇时，歧视者的意图和动机变得无关紧要，因为行为的“理由”是不言自明的。相反，在诸如纳加拉贾和本案涉及A机构的案件中，拒绝

the "ground" of the action is self-explanatory. On the contrary, in cases such as Nagarajan and the present case concerning Amnesty, the denial of appointment and promotion is not in itself discriminatory, which is why the court had to deduce the alleged discriminator's motivation, the so called "mental processes". In the present case it was fairly obvious that the motivation behind Amnesty denying the claimant of her promotion was "on grounds" of race, which Underhill J believes to be all that is necessary to establish direct discrimination. The respondent's argument that they did so with benign motives and intention is, in Underhill J's judgment, irrelevant. Underhill J expressly stated in his conclusion that in cases where the courts are forced to deduce the motivation behind the act, *"It is important to bear in mind that the subject of the inquiry is the ground of, or reason for, the putative discriminator's action, not his motive."*

To recapitulate the centre of Underhill J's position on this matter: there exists occasions where the courts must draw inferences behind the motives of the alleged discriminator, yet once the motives are found to be racially motivated, whether benign or not, would be liable for direct discrimination. Underhill J drew a line between the "grounds" of discrimination and the "intentions" of discrimination, and argued that once the former has been established, the latter becomes irrelevant. To use Underhill J's words, *"it is, we believe, clear that Mr Epstein's submission set out at para 26 above is misconceived. There is no 'two-stage approach' such as he propounds. The only question for the tribunal was whether the*

任命和晋升本身并不是歧视性的，这就是为什么法院必须推断出歧视者的动机，即所谓的“心理过程”。本案中，相当明显的是，A机构拒绝申请人晋升的动机是“基于”种族，昂德希尔法官认为知道这点后，确立直接歧视已经足够。在昂德希尔法官的判断中，被申请人的论点，即他们这样做的动机和意图是善意的，均是无关的。昂德希尔法官在其结论中明确指出，在法院被迫推断行为背后的动机的情况下，“重要的是要铭记，调查的主体是推断歧视者的行为的理由，而不是其动机”。

对昂德希尔法官在这一问题上的中心立场的概括：在有些情况下，法院必须根据所指控的歧视者的动机作出推断，但无论其动机是否出于善意，一旦发现动机是出于种族，就会成为直接歧视。昂德希尔法官在歧视的“理由”和歧视的“意图”之间划了一条线，并认为一旦前者确立，后者就变得无关紧要。用昂德希尔法官的话来说，“我们认为，爱泼斯坦先生在上文第26段中提出的意见显然是错误的，不存在他所提出的‘两阶段’。法庭面临的唯一问题是，A机构决定不任命申请人为苏丹研究员的理由或原因是否为她的族裔血统”。

ground of, or reason for, A Institution's decision not to appoint the claimant as Sudan researcher was her ethnic origins."

Ultimately, the Employment Appeal Tribunal upheld the previous decision that there was direct discrimination found in A Institution's denial of promotion.

Comments

The significant point to take away from this case decision is the distinction between "grounds" and "intentions". Once it has been discovered that the claimant was subjected to less favourable treatment because of his race, it is completely irrelevant why such treatment occurred. Though it may get confusing at certain occasions, it is helpful to remember that only the objective reason is relevant, but not what subjectively motivates the alleged discriminator.

Today's society is one where discrimination occurs daily, a despicable form of hostility. While it is certainty recognizable that some discriminatory actions are not ill-advised, it is crucial that direct discrimination remains largely unjustifiable, in order to offer the best possible form of protection.

最后，就业上诉法庭维持了先前的裁决，即 A 机构拒绝晋升存在直接歧视。

案件评述

本案判决的重要一点，是区分“理由”和“意图”。一旦发现申请人因其种族而受到劣于待遇，发生这种待遇背后的意图就完全无关紧要。虽然在某些情况下这可能令人困惑，但需要记住只有客观原因是相关的，而不是涉案歧视者的主观动机。

如今每天都在发生歧视，这是一种恶意行为。虽然可以肯定的是，有些歧视行为并非不明智的，但至关重要的是，为了提供最好的保护形式，直接歧视在很大程度上仍然是不能被证明正当的。

Case 2 Homer v Chief Constable of West Yorkshire —Indirect discrimination and its justification

Preface:

Discrimination appears in many forms, the last article on direct discrimination merely covered one. When one mentions discrimination, it becomes an inescapable task to explore the essence of equality. Direct discrimination in the last article strives to achieve what is called "formal equality", where everyone must be treated equally, with the identical treatments applying to every comparable individual. Though this may not always suffice, as in certain circumstances individuals may possess qualities which require additional care or treatments. Policies which may prima facie be equal to all are in fact discriminatory to specific persons, which invokes the necessity to carry out different treatments and policies to those in need. Disputes frequently arise from those occasions and are often referred to in English Law as "Indirect Discrimination".

案例 2　霍尔默诉西约克郡警察局局长案
——间接歧视及其正当性

引言：

歧视有多种形式，上一篇文章涉及的直接歧视只是其中一种。每当提到歧视，就不可避免地需要探究平等的本质。上篇的直接歧视问题中，力求实现所谓的“形式上的平等”，即每个人都必须得到平等的对待，对每个可比个体都要适用同样的待遇。但是这并不足以消除歧视，因为在某些情况下，个别人可能具有需要额外呵护或对待的特质。表面上对所有人平等的政策实际上对特定的人是具有歧视性的，这就导致有必要对有特殊需要的人实行不同的待遇和政策。这些情形经常会引起争议，在英国法律中被称为“间接歧视”。

Facts

The claimant Mr Homer retired from the police force when he was 51 years old and subsequently joined the Police National Legal Database (PNLD) as a legal adviser. At the time of his appointment there were no additional requirements on degrees, and the claimant was appointed due to his experience in the police force and his knowledge in Criminal law. Though years later, when the claimant has reached 62 years of age the police constable, in an attempt to attract younger, more suitable candidates and to retain experienced employees, introduced a new pay grade structure in PNLD where persons who do not hold a law degree cannot enter the top pay grade as they do not meet the criteria.

This was terrible news for Mr Homer since the retirement age in the PNLD was 65, meaning he would have less than 3 years to obtain a law degree if he wishes to reach the highest pay grade by the time of his retirement. This is, however, impossible to achieve since obtaining a law degree by part-time study would take at least four years. Mr Homer claimed that there was indirect age discrimination by the Police Constable.

Issue

What are the mandatory requirements of indirect discrimination? And how can one attempt to justify a case of indirect discrimination?

案件事实

申请人霍尔默先生 51 岁时从警察部队退休，随后加入国家警察法律数据库 (PNLD) 担任法律顾问。他被任命时没有关于学位的额外要求，其任命是出于他在警察部队的经验和刑法方面的知识。但是在几年后，当申请人年满 62 岁时，警察局局长为了吸引更年轻、更合适的候选人并同时留住有经验的雇员，在 PNLD 部门采用了新的薪级结构，没有法律学位的员工不能进入最高薪级，因为他们不符合标准。

这对霍尔默先生来说是个很坏的消息，因为 PNLD 规定的退休年龄是 65 岁。这意味着，如果他希望在退休时达到最高工资级别，只有不到 3 年的时间获得法律学位。然而，这是不可能实现的，因为通过非全日制学习获得法律学位至少需要 4 年时间。霍尔默先生诉称警察局局长存在间接的年龄歧视。

争议焦点

间接歧视有哪些强制性规定？一个人如何能够试图证明间接歧视的正当性？

Judicial View

The Law:

Before analysing the judgments by the relevant courts and tribunals, it is essential to first understand the basics of indirect discrimination in the UK:

Regulation 3 of the Employment Equality (Age) Regulations 2006 states that:

"(1) For the purposes of these Regulations, a person ('A') discriminates against another person ('B') if— ... (b) A applies to B a provision, criterion or practice which he applies or would apply equally to persons not of the same age group as B, but— (i) which puts or would put persons of the same age group as B at a particular disadvantage when compared with other persons, and (ii) which puts B at that disadvantage, and A cannot show the ... provision, criterion or practice to be a proportionate means of achieving a legitimate aim."

Three factors are to be considered:

Provision, criterion or practice (PCP): The employer must have introduced a PCP which has power over all employees, including those that share the same characteristics with the claimant and those who do not.

Particular disadvantage: The PCP may be equal on its surface, but would put certain individuals, who share the same

司法观点

法律条文：

在分析相关法院和法庭的判决之前，我们必须首先了解英国间接歧视的基础概念：

《2006年就业平等（年龄）条例》第3条规定：

（1）就本规例而言，任何人（“A”）歧视另一人（“B”），如——……（b）A向B适用一项规定、标准或做法，而该规定、标准或做法是他适用于或将会平等地适用于与B并非同一年龄组别的人的，但——（i）将会使与B相同年龄组的人处于或将处于与其他人相比的特殊不利地位，以及（ii）使B处于该不利地位，并且A不能表明……规定、标准或做法是实现合法目的的适当手段。

须考虑的三个因素：

规定、标准或做法（PCP）：雇主必须引入PCP，且该PCP对所有员工具有效力，包括与申请人具有相同特征的员工和不具有相同特征的员工。

特别的不利之处：该PCP表面上可能是平等的，但会使与申请人具有相同特征的某些人处于比不具有相同特征的人更不

characteristics with the claimant in situations less favourable than those who do not.

Justification: The most distinct feature of indirect-discrimination, that it can be justified, given that the PCP in question must be an appropriate and no more than necessary means to reach a legitimate aim, namely the renowned "Proportionality" doctrine.

Employment Tribunal:

The first instance judge ruled in Mr Homer's favour and argued that the age group which was particularly disadvantaged was people aged 60 to 65 years of age, who would not be able to obtain a law degree before the retirement age of 65. The judge stated that the PCP introduced by the respondent police constable put employees in this age group in less favourable positions when compared with other employees who are younger and who still have much time to reach the highest pay grade.

The Employment Appeal Tribunal and the Court of Appeal:

However, the chief constable appealed against the first instance decision and the case subsequently reached the Employment Appeal Tribunal (EAT) and the Court of Appeal (CA) the second and third instance courts were satisfied that indirect discrimination were not established since it was not Mr Homer's age which rendered

利的处境。

正当性：间接歧视最明显的特征在于，如果所涉及的 PCP 是达到合法目的的适当且必要手段，则其可被认定具有正当性，即著名的“相称性”原则。

就业法庭：

一审法官判定霍尔默先生胜诉，认为处于特别不利地位的年龄组是 60~65 岁的人，他们将无法在 65 岁退休之前获得法律学位。法官指出，与其他年龄较小且仍有大量时间达到最高工资等级的员工相比，被申请人警察局局长引入的 PCP 使该年龄组的员工处于劣势 地位。

就业上诉法庭及上诉法院：

然而，警察局局长对一审判决提出上诉，案件随后提交就业上诉法庭（EAT）和上诉法院（CA），二审和三审法院认为，间接歧视不成立，因为霍尔默先生的年龄并不是导致他无法获得法律学位的原因，而是因为他即将退休。代表雇主的刘易斯先生认为，第 3（1）（b）条中“使处在”的措辞表明，必须

him impossible to obtain the law degree, but instead was his impending retirement. Mr Lewis, who represented the employer argued that the diction of "puts at" in regulation 3(1)(b) indicates that one must explore the real "perpetrator" behind Mr Homer's inability to reach the highest grade, and that it is not his age, but his retirement. Mr Lewis further argued that the employees who are under similar circumstances with Mr Homer are not those who are between the age of 60-65, but those, whether young or old, are nearing retirement for whatever reasons. For instance, people who are forced to retire due to family reasons. This, as Mr Lewis argued will not constitute indirect discrimination under the Employment Equality (Age) Regulations 2006 since age is not the reason, but rather the proximity of retirement. This was accepted by the EAT and the CA. Though the EAT also held that if indirect discrimination were to be found, the discriminatory act would not be able to be justified.

The supreme court:

The claimant, Mr Homer appealed to the Supreme Court against the second and third instance decision that there was no indirect discrimination to be found and the respondent Chief Constable (PNLD) cross appealed on the EAT's point that if there were discrimination found it would not be justified. Baroness Hale, opened her judgment with, *"taking the particular disadvantage which is suffered by a particular age group for a reason which is*

探究霍尔默先生无法达到最高等级背后真正的“肇事者”，不是他的年龄，而是他即将退休。刘易斯先生进一步指出，与霍尔默先生处境相似的员工并不是年龄在60~65岁的员工，而是那些无论是年轻还是年老，不管出于何种原因，均接近退休的员工。例如，由于家庭原因被迫退休的人。正如刘易斯先生所说，这不会构成《2006年就业平等（年龄）条例》中规定的间接歧视，因为年龄不是原因，而是退休的临近程度。就业上诉法庭和上诉法院均接受了这一观点。但是，就业上诉法庭也认为，如果间接歧视被确立，那么该歧视行为将是不正当的。

最高法院：

申请人霍尔默先生向最高法院提出上诉，反对二审和三审关于不存在间接歧视的裁决。被申请人警察局局长（PNLD）也提出上诉，不认可就业上诉法庭认为如果存在歧视则不构成正当性的观点。黑尔女大法官在判决开始时说道：**“将某一年龄组因与其年龄有关的原因而遭受的特殊不利条件与其他人因与其年龄无关的完全不同的原因而遭受的类似不利条件等同……将对歧视法产生令人震惊的后果。”**她在此发言后举例说，不

related to their age and equating it with a similar disadvantage which is suffered by others but for a completely different reason unrelated to their age... would have alarming consequences for the law of discrimination." She followed her statement with an example that, one cannot say that a PCP which requires all employees to grow beards is not discriminatory against women simply because there are men who cannot grow a beard.

Baroness Hale submitted that people who retire for family reasons are often given the choice to do so after obtaining the law degree, since they usually have the benefit of time, while people such as Mr Homer lack such opportunities. Furthermore, regulation 30 of the Age Regulations provided that employers are not required to justify the decision to retire an employee at the age of 65, signifying that Mr Homer may be facing mandatory retirement in 3 years.

Baroness Hale then moved on to address the concern that whether Mr Homer would be asking for more favourable treatment for him and employees in their age, which would in turn be potentially discriminatory for the younger population. She rejected this theory and cited the case *London Underground Ltd v Edwards (No 2) [1999] ICR 494*, where a new roster for underground train drivers were indirectly discriminatory on the ground of sex as it had more impacts on single parents, which were predominantly female. Baroness Hale explained that in this case the problem was not solved by making exceptions for the women, but by providing benefits for single parents of any sex. This may be applied also to

能仅仅因为有些男性天生不长胡须，而认为要求所有雇员留胡须的 PCP 不歧视女性。

黑尔女大法官认为，由于家庭原因而退休的人通常可以在获得法律学位后再选择退休，因为他们通常有时间的优势，而像霍尔默先生这样的人则缺乏这样的机会。此外，《2006 年就业平等（年龄）条例》第 30 条规定，雇主无须证明使雇员在 65 岁退休的决定是正当的，这意味着霍尔默先生可能在 3 年内面临强制性退休。

黑尔女大法官接着谈到，霍尔默先生是否会要求对他和同龄雇员给予更优待遇的问题，反而可能对年轻人造成歧视。她驳斥了这一理论，并引用了伦敦地铁有限公司诉爱德华兹案（第 2 号）（[1999] ICR 494），其中地铁司机的新值勤表被判定是基于性别的间接歧视，因为它对以女性为主的单身父母影响更大。黑尔女大法官解释说，在这种情况下，解决问题的办法不是将女性视为例外，而是为任何性别的单身父母提供福利。这也适用于本案，任何即将退休的雇员都可以获得某些福利，霍尔默先生也包括在内。

the current case, where any employees nearing retirement may be provided with certain benefits, Mr Homer included.

To summarize her arguments on indirect age discrimination, Baroness Hale stated: *"the reason for the disadvantage was that people in this age group did not have time to acquire a law degree. And the reason why they did not have time to acquire a law degree was that they were soon to reach the age of retirement."*

Justification:

Since the Chief Constable cross appealed against the point on the matter that if the act were held to be discriminatory, it would not be justified, Baroness Hale addressed the problems concerning justification.

As mentioned before, one of the unique features of indirect discrimination is that it can potentially be justified, provided that the PCP is a proportionate means of achieving a legitimate aim. Baroness Hale cited the three-step test derived by Mummery LJ in *Elias [2006] 1 WLR 3213*:

"First, is the objective sufficiently important to justify limiting a fundamental right? Secondly, is the measure rationally connected to the objective? Thirdly, are the means chosen no more than is necessary to accomplish the objective?"

Baroness Hale then proceeded to analyse the case in question, where she first stated that PNLD's aim for the law degree requirement was *"to facilitate the recruitment and retention of the*

黑尔女大法官在总结她关于间接年龄歧视的论点时说："不利产生的原因是这个年龄段的人没有时间获得法律学位。而他们没有时间获得法律学位的原因是他们很快就要到退休年龄。"

正当性：

由于警察局局长对如果认定该行为具有歧视性，则该行为将没有正当性的观点提出上诉，黑尔女大法官对有关正当性的问题做出了回应。

如前所述，间接歧视的一个特点是，只要 PCP 是实现正当目的的适当措施，它就有可能成为正当手段。黑尔女大法官引用了迈莫里大法官在伊莱亚斯案（[2006] 1 WLR 3213）中得出的三步验证标准：

> 第一，目标是否足够重要，足以证明限制一项基本权利是正当的？第二，该措施是否与目标有合理的联系？第三，所选择的手段是否不超过实现目标所必需的限度？

黑尔女大法官接着分析了本案，她首先指出，PNLD 对法律学位要求的目的是"便利 PNLD 聘用和保留具有适当能力的工作人员"。她提出，必须区分 PNLD 聘用或保留新工作人

staff of appropriate calibre with the PNLD." She argued that it is imperative to distinguish between PNLD's aim of recruiting or retaining new staff and retaining existing staff who were employed under a different grading system. Baroness Hale thought that while it was highly possible that the requirement of a law degree would elevate the calibre of new recruits, it is not absolute that this would motivate or encourage existing employees to stay by such an incentive. She cited *Hennigs v Eisenbahn-Bundesamt [2012] 1 CMLR 484* and stated that introducing age related pay scales is not an appropriate means to reward experience, since it is not certain that all older employees are more experienced than the young. Therefore, Baroness Halequestioned whether PNLD's enforcement of the law degreerequirement is appropriate to retain existing employees such as Mr Homer, and whether their aim of recruiting better employees may be achieved instead by limiting this degree requirement to only exist at the recruitment stage.

The Supreme Court reached a unanimous decision and held that Mr Homer was indirectly discriminated against by the Police Constable on the ground of age. The matter on justification was remitted for further consideration by the Employment Tribunal.

Comments

The essence of the treatment to this case came from the overwhelmingly informative and insightful judgment from Baroness Hale, which aided the legal community on its whole understanding

员的目的和保留在不同薪级制度下雇用的现有工作人员的目的。黑尔女大法官认为，虽然对法律学位的要求极有可能会提高新雇员的水平，但这并非绝对会激励或鼓励现有雇员继续留任。她引用了亨尼格斯诉德国联邦铁路局案（[2012] 1 CMLR 484），并指出引入与年龄相关的薪资标准并不是奖励工作经验的适当手段，因为不能确定所有年长员工都比年轻员工更有经验。因此，黑尔女大法官质疑 PNLD 执行法律学位的要求是否适合留住霍尔默先生这样的现有员工，以及是否可以通过限制该学位要求仅存在于招聘阶段而实现其招聘更好员工的目的。

最高法院达成一致裁决，认为霍尔默先生受到警察局局长基于年龄的间接歧视。关于正当性的问题已转交就业法庭进一步审议。

案件评述

这个案件处理的精华来自黑尔女大法官所提供的信息量极大且见解极为深刻的判决，其有助于法律界对间接歧视的整体理解。

of indirect discrimination.

The essential points to remember from this case is that the Supreme court clarified that courts are not willing to accept technical arguments such as the "proximity of retirement" in the current case. The central dispute of any indirect discrimination cases rests in the "justification" section, where proportionality remains a problematic doctrine to apply. An interesting point to think about is the Supreme court's decision to remit the case back to the ET considering justification, where it is questionable why they did not address the decision themselves. It is possible that the Supreme court was worried that making an exception for Mr Homer would affect future case decisions as this may introduce another layer of discrimination against other groups.

Finally, since indirect discrimination cases begs the question as to what the ultimate form of equality is the society wishes to achieve, is it formal equality, which hopes to apply the identical standard and treatment to every individual, or is substantive equality more preferable, where it is imperative to treat groups of individual more favourable when necessary.

从本案中需要记住的要点是，最高法院澄清，法院不愿意采纳诸如本案中“接近退休”等技术性论点。任何间接歧视案件的核心争议均在于“理由的正当性”这一环节，在该环节中，如何适用“相称性”原则仍旧存在争议 。一个值得思考的有趣之处是，最高法院为什么决定将案件发回就业法庭去审议正当性，而不是亲自处理。最高法院可能担心为霍尔默先生破例会影响未来的案件判决，因为这可能给其他群体带来另一层歧视。

最后，间接歧视案件引出了一个问题，即社会希望实现的最终平等形式是什么，是希望对每个人适用相同标准和待遇的形式平等，还是实质平等更为可取，即必要时必须对某些群体给予更有利的待遇。

Case 3 Richmond Ltd v Dhaliwal
—Harassment and objective sensitivity

Preface:

The last two articles analysed two traditional forms of discrimination, where individuals were targeted and received less favourable treatments due to their different characteristics. However, discrimination also involves harassment, a hostile form of behaviour which is unfortunately frequent, especially in employment. The main difficulty surrounding harassment is the complexity of analysing one's mental state, since in certain occasions a sentence not meant to cause any harm may constitute "harassment" in the victim's mind. Different individuals possess distinct level of sensitivity to remarks made by others, which poses a real difficulty to judges who wish to respect the rights of both parties.

Facts

The claimant, Ms Dhaliwal was an employee in the respondent company, Richmond Pharmacology Ltd. She is British but is of

案例 3　里士满公司诉达里瓦尔案
——骚扰与客观敏感性

引言：

前两篇文章对两种传统形式的歧视作出了分析，在该两种歧视中，个人因其不同的特点而成为歧视的目标并受到劣于他人的待遇。然而，歧视还涉及骚扰行为，不幸的是，这是一种频发的，特别是在就业领域频发的敌意行为。与认定骚扰相关的主要困难在于分析一个人主观精神状态的复杂性，因为在某些情况下，一些不具有伤害目的的语言可能在受害者的心中构成“骚扰”。不同的人对他人的言论具有不同程度的敏感性，这给希望尊重双方权利的法官带来了一定的困难。

案件事实

申请人达里瓦尔女士是被申请人公司里士满药物有限公司的一名雇员。她是英国人，但具有印度裔血统。达里瓦尔女士

Indian ethnic origin. Ms Dhaliwal has been employed for 5 years and since been promoted to project manager. It was found upon the facts that she had always been excellent at her job and formed pleasant working relationships with her managers, especially Dr Lorch, who was one of the founding members of the company.

The claimant gave one month's notice of resignation on August 13, 2007, and it was to the judges' knowledge that this made the company, including Dr Lorch relatively upset since they expected Ms Dhaliwal to give a minimum of two months' notice considering that she was in a senior position. Due to this inconvenience, Dr Lorch asked the claimant to remain at work during a tube strike, and it was in Dr Lorch's perception that since then Ms Dhaliwal's work quality began to fall off.

A short meeting took place between the two individuals on September 3, 2007, where Dr Lorch made clear to the claimant that her work began to deteriorate. At the end of the discussion Dr Lorch allegedly said to the claimant, *"We will probably bump into each other in future, unless you are married off in India." The respondent insisted that what was said in reality by Dr Lorch was "married, or in India". The claimant was infuriated and claimed racial harassment against the company.*

Issue

How does an act constitute harassment in an employment context? And how can it be justified?

在工作了5年后被提升为项目经理。事实证明，她在工作上一直表现出色，并与她的管理人员，特别是公司创始成员之一的洛奇博士建立了愉快的工作关系。

申请人于2007年8月13日提前一个月递交了辞职通知，据法官所知，这使包括洛奇博士在内的公司人员颇感不悦，因为考虑到达里瓦尔女士处于高级职位，他们希望她至少提前两个月发出辞职通知。由于这个情况造成的不便，洛奇博士要求申请人在地铁罢工期间继续工作，而在洛奇博士看来，从那时起达里瓦尔女士的工作质量开始下降。

2007年9月3日，两人进行了一次简短的会面，洛奇博士向申请人明确表示，她的工作质量开始下降。据申请人所称，在讨论结束时，洛奇博士对申请人说："除非你回印度结婚，否则我们将来很可能碰面。"被申请人坚持认为洛奇博士所说的是"除非你已婚，或在印度"。申请人被这句话激怒，诉称公司对她进行了种族上的骚扰。

争议焦点

在雇佣环境中，什么行为会构成骚扰？它怎么能被证明是正当的？

Judicial View

The Law:

The law regarding harassment is slightly different from direct and indirect discrimination. Therefore, it is imperative one understands its basics:

Subject to section 3A of the Race Relations Act 1976:

"(1) A person subjects another to harassment...where, on grounds of race or ethnic or national origins, he engages in unwanted conduct which has the purpose or effect of—(a) violating that otherperson's dignity, or (b) creating an intimidating, hostile, degrading, humiliating or offensive environment for him. (2) Conduct shall be regarded as having the effect specified in paragraph (a) or (b) of subsection (1) only if, having regard to all the circumstances, including in particular the perception of that other person, it should reasonably be considered as having that effect."

To simplify, this section may be divided into the following elements:

1. The unwanted conduct: There must be an action, conducted by the respondent which is unwanted by the claimant.

2. The purpose or effect: The unwanted conduct must have the purpose, or effect to (a) violate dignity or (b) create an intimidating, hostile, degrading, humiliating or offensive environment for the claimant.

3. The grounds for the conduct: The claimant's race must be

司法观点

法律条文：

关于骚扰的法律要求与直接和间接歧视略有不同。因此，我们必须了解其基础概念：

根据《1976 年种族关系法》第 3A 条：

（1）任何人使另一人受到骚扰…… 如该人基于种族、族裔或民族血统而做出不受欢迎的行为，其目的或效果是——（a）侵犯该另一人的尊严，或（b）对其制造恐吓、敌意、有辱人格、羞辱或冒犯的环境。（2）只有在考虑到所有情况，特别是该另一人的感受，将被合理地认为具有该等效果，该行为才应被视为具有（a）或（b）段所指出的效果。

为简化起见，该条款可分为以下要素：

1. 不受欢迎的行为：须存在被申请人做出的不受申请人欢迎的行为。

2. 目的或效果：该不受欢迎的行为必须具有以下目的或效果：（a）侵犯尊严，或（b）对申请人制造一种恐吓、敌意、有辱人格、羞辱或冒犯的环境。

3. 行为的理由：申请人的种族必须是骚扰背后的动机。

the motivation behind the harassment.

4. Reasonableness: It must be reasonable for the claimant to feel his or her dignity violated or been put in an intimidating environment.

The employment tribunal (ET):

The first instance judges held that while the remark itself was not necessarily meant to be offensive, it had however amounted to an unwanted conduct and had violated the claimant's dignity. The Tribunal further held that it would make little difference whether Dr Lorch said "married off in India" or "married, or in India" as both versions of the remark would hint towards the stereotype of marriage for women in India. From these reasons the Tribunal upheld the complaint and held that Dr Lorch's words constituted harassment under section 3A of the 1976 Act. The Claimant, Ms. Dhaliwal was awarded 1000 pounds for injury to feelings. The respondent, Richmond Ltd appealed to the Employment Appeal Tribunal where the matter was reconsidered.

The Employment Appeal Tribunal (EAT):

Underhill J began his judgment with a careful consideration of certain elements in section 3A of the 1976 Act. He stated that the requirement of "purpose" and "effect" are equally as important and does not depend on one another for the constitution of harassment.

4. 合理性：申请人感到自己的尊严受到侵犯或处于令人恐惧的环境必须是合理的。

就业法庭（ET）:

一审法官认为，虽然这句话本身并不一定具有冒犯性，但它构成了一种不受欢迎的行为，并且侵犯了申请人的尊严。法庭进一步认为，洛奇博士所说的“回印度结婚”或“已婚，或在印度”没有什么区别，因为这两种说法都暗示了对于印度妇女婚姻的刻板印象。基于这些原因，法庭支持了诉求，并认为洛奇博士的言论构成了《1976 年种族关系法》第 3A 条规定的骚扰。申请人达里瓦尔女士因情绪受伤被判给 1000 英镑。被申请人里士满公司向就业上诉法庭提出上诉，该法庭重新审议了此案。

就业上诉法庭 (EAT):

昂德希尔法官在开始判决时，仔细考虑了《1976 年种族关系法》第 3A 条中的某些要素。他指出：“目的”和“效果”的要求同等重要，在构成骚扰时并不相互依赖。这意味着，如果歧视者怀有善意动机，却制造了敌意环境或侵犯了申请人的尊

This signifies that if the discriminator carries benign motives, but nonetheless created a hostile environment or violated the claimant's dignity, harassment would be found. Conversely, the discriminator will also be held liable if he carried hostile motives to harass but did not in reality cause any harm towards the claimant. Underhill J further reinforced the idea that courts are more inclined to focus on the effect of the conduct in question since there were few cases where the respondent intended to bring upon negative consequences but failed to do so.

The primary focus of the analysis was on the "reasonableness" test, namely whether it was reasonable for the claimant to feel that her dignity was violated. Mr Majumdar, who represented the respondent argued that this was a controversial and difficult section as it was unclear whether the reasonable test was objective or subjective. The diction used in section 3A (2)(1), *"including in particular the perception of that other person"* may suggest that the test was a subjective one. However, Underhill J argued that this was rather straightforward, as he stated, *"the victim must have felt, or perceived, her dignity to have been violated or an adverse environment to have been created. That can, if you like, be described as introducing a 'subjective' element; but overall the criterion is objective because what the tribunal is required to consider is whether, if the claimant has experienced those feelings or perceptions, it was reasonable for her to do so."* As the test is clarified to be an objective one, both the purpose and effect of the unwanted remark should be taken into consideration by the

严，就会构成骚扰。相反，如果歧视者怀有敌意动机进行骚扰，但实际上没有对申请人造成任何损害，他也将承担责任。昂德希尔法官进一步强调了这样一种观点，即法院更倾向于关注所涉行为的效果，因为很少出现被申请人意图造成负面后果却未成功的案例。

法官分析的重点是“合理性”验证标准，即申请人认为其尊严受到侵犯是否合理。代表被申请人的马宗达先生认为，这是一个有争议且困难的条文，因为不清楚合理性验证标准是客观的还是主观的。第 3A（2）（1）条中使用的措辞“尤其包括该另一人的感受”，可能表明该标准是主观验证标准。然而，昂德希尔法官认为，这相当简单，正如他所说，“受害者必须感到或感觉到她的尊严将受到侵犯或不利的环境将会产生；这也确实能被称作是主观的。但总的来说，这一标准是客观的，因为法庭需要考虑的是，如果申请人经历过这些感受或看法，她这样做是否合理”。由于该验证标准被澄清为一个客观的判断标准，法庭就应当考虑该不受欢迎的言论的目的和效果。

Tribunal.

The respondents produced several and over-elaborated grounds of appeal, Underhill J had since summarized it down to 3 primary points:

1. As the ET stated, there was no intention or purpose by Dr Lorch to violate the claimant's dignity.

2. The ET did not expressly state that the remark hinted towards the stereotype of "forced marriage", instead the remark may have instead be referring to arranged marriages, which would be less offensive, since it was stated in the facts that the claimant had communicated the idea of getting an arranged marriage to Dr Lorch before. Moreover, the Tribunal stated that the differentiation between "married off" and "married, or" was inconsequential, yet it was in fact crucial to any perception, meaning the Tribunal did not base its decision on the specific wording of the remark.

3. The remark should have failed the reasonableness test as it could not have reasonably violated the claimant's dignity, considering that the "violation of dignity" was inherently a strong phrase and should carry with it a high threshold.

To respond the said grounds of appeal, Underhill J stated that while the respondent was correct in stating that the ET did not expressly state the words "forced marriage", it was sufficient upon the facts that Dr Lorch was indeed trying to invoke the stereotype of forced marriage in India. He further argued, it was inconsequential what the ET's position was on the differentiation between "married off" and "married, or" since the EAT concurs with the ET on

被申请人提出了几个过于详细的上诉理由，昂德希尔法官随后将其归纳为三个要点：

1. 如就业法庭所述，洛奇博士并没有侵犯申请人尊严的意图或目的。

2. 就业法庭没有明确指出，这句话暗示了“强迫婚姻”的刻板印象，相反，这句话可能是指包办婚姻，这种说法不会那么令人反感，而事实上申请人以前曾与洛奇博士交流过获得包办婚姻的想法。此外，法庭指出，“回去结婚”与“已婚，或”之间的区别无关紧要，但实际上任何人都会认为这至关重要，这意味着法庭的裁决并非以该评论的具体措辞为依据。

3. 这句话本应无法通过合理性验证标准，因为合理来讲，这不可能侵犯申请人的尊严，考虑到“侵犯尊严”一词本身就是一个强有力的词组，其应当附带一个很高的标准。

为了回应上述上诉理由，昂德希尔法官说，虽然如被申请人所说，就业法庭的确没有明确说明“强迫婚姻”一词，但事实足够表明，洛奇博士确实在试图提起印度强迫婚姻的刻板印象。他进一步指出，就业法庭在区分“回去结婚”和“已婚，或”方面的立场是无关紧要的，因为就业上诉法庭同意就业法庭的观点，即两个版本都明确提及强迫婚姻和对印度人的刻板印象。昂德希尔法官的结论是，根据上述调查结果，法庭确信

the point that both versions would be clearly referring to forced marriages and stereotypes towards the Indian population. Underhill J concluded his judgment that from the above findings the Tribunal was satisfied that the remark in question passed the reasonableness test and held that there was harassment found on the part of the respondent and the appeal was dismissed.

Comments

The essence of this case comes from its position on reasonableness and its application in practice. As the EAT confirmed, while the feeling of the claimant and the effect was the primary focus of any harassment case, it was up to the courts and tribunals to apply an objective test, questioning the conduct and whether it was reasonable that the said effects were placed upon the claimant. This is nonetheless a troublesome test to apply, as it was vital to the operation of the employment environment and any other environments to protect the rights and well-being of each individual while not creating a hyper-sensitive population easily offended by any conducts.

有关言论通过了合理性验证标准，并认为被申请人对申请人构成骚扰，上诉被驳回。

案件评述

本案的核心在于其对合理性的立场及其在实践中的运用。正如就业上诉法庭所确认的，虽然申请人的感受及其效果是任何骚扰案件的主要焦点，但应由法院和法庭采用客观验证标准进行评判，并质疑所述行为以及前述效果施加于申请人是否合理。然而，这依旧是一个问题重重的验证标准，因为就业环境或任何其他环境运行的关键在于，既要保护每个人的权利和福祉，又要避免形成易受任何行为冒犯的高度敏感人群。

Part Four: Selected Cases under Labour Law

第四部分：劳动法案例

案例 1　卡迈克尔诉国家电力公司案

[1999] 1 W.L.R. 2042

案例 2　莱恩诉夏尔屋顶（牛津）有限公司案

[1995] P.I.Q.R. P417

案例 3　优步公司诉阿斯拉姆案

[2021] R.T.R. 29

Case 1 Carmichael v National Power Plc
—To be, or not to be, an employee

Preface:

The law on employment status has always had consistent questions that have been countered by the most inconsistent of answers. Over the history of labour law, the English court has developed a multiplicity of tests on whether one is in law under a "contract of service", such as the "control" test and the "economic reality" test, though it was never stated expressly on which is to be the authoritative rule. This issue remains in the mist of uncertainty.

However, there are judges who displayed intellectual processes of critical thinking which could aid the clarification of employment status, the current case decided by the House of Lords may be considered as one.

Facts

The applicants, Mrs Leese and Mrs Carmichael saw an advertisement posted by the respondent company, C.E.G.B. during

案例 1　卡迈克尔诉国家电力公司案
——是否成为员工

引言:

关于雇佣身份的法律总是存在问题，而这些问题却一直得不到一致的答案。在劳动法的历史上，英国法院对一个人是否在法律上存在“服务合同”形成了多种验证标准，如“控制”验证标准和“经济现实”验证标准，却从未明确规定哪一项才是权威规则。该问题仍处于不确定的迷雾中。

然而，有些法官展现出了批判性思维的智力过程，这有助于澄清雇佣身份问题，上议院裁定的这一案件可被视为其中之一。

案件事实

申请人莱斯夫人和卡迈克尔夫人看到了被申请人公司C.E.G.B. 在 1988 年 11 月发布的一则广告（以下简称 1989 年

November 1988 ("the 1989 documentation"), which stated, *"for the posts of station guides", "Successful candidates"* would be required to *"Supervise parties of visitors on pre-selected tour routes around the power station site..."* At the end of the description, the document stated, *"Employment will be on a casual as required basis."*

The applicants applied, and were interviewed for the position of tour guides and were both successful as they received the following letter:

"I am pleased to note that you are agreeable to be employed by the C.E.G.B. ... On a casual as required basis... When your services are required."

The end of the letter again emphasized on the nature of the employment: *"Casual Employment, casual as required."*

Both ladies were subsequently trained and worked as guides when they were available and chose to accept the work, the language of "employment" was used, and they were in fact on the payroll just as any other employees.

During 1995, the two applicants brought an action to the industrial tribunal that they had not received the written statements of their employment status as required under section 1 of the Employment Rights Act 1996. This is where the main issue arose, since it necessitated them to establish that they were in fact and in law employees of C.E.G.B.

文件），其中写道，“关于车站导游的职位”，“成功的候选人”将被要求“监督参观团参观预先选定的发电站周围的路线”。在描述的末尾，该文件指出，“将根据需要临时雇用”。

两位申请人申请并面试了导游职位且均获得成功，她们收到了以下信函：

> 我很高兴地通知，C.E.G.B 同意聘用您……在需要您的服务时……基于临时需要。

信末再次强调了雇佣的性质，“在临时要求时予以临时雇佣”。

这两位女士后来均接受了培训，当她们有时间并选择接受这项工作时，她们就从事向导工作，工作中也存在“雇佣”一词，而且事实上和其他雇员一样，她们在工资单上。

1995 年，两名申请人在劳资争议法庭提起诉讼，称她们没有收到《1996 年就业权利法》第 1 条所要求的关于其雇佣身份的书面陈述。本案的主要问题就出现在此处，因为她们必须确定事实上和在法律上她们是 C.E.G.B. 的雇员。

Issue

What are the requirements in order to be recognized in law as employees?

Judicial View

The industrial tribunal decision:

The first instance court held that the case at hand *"founders on the rock of absence of mutuality,"* that when the respondent company did not require any work to be done, there were no contractual relationships between the applicants and C.E.G.B. in any form.

The tribunal founded their finding on three major points:

1. The language adopted by C.E.G.B. on the 1989 documentation;
2. The way in which it was operated;
3. The evidence of the parties on how it was understood.

From the facts the tribunal was satisfied that they were not under any contract of employment due to the lack of mutuality of obligations, since there was no obligation on the part of the company to provide work and there were no obligations by the applicants to undertake work when it was made available. The applicants appealed against this decision and the matter reached the court of appeal.

争议焦点

在法律上被承认为雇员有什么条件?

司法观点

劳资争议法庭判决:

一审法院认为,本案“*在撞到缺乏相互性这一巨石后沉没*”,即当被申请人公司不需要其做任何工作时,两位申请人与C.E.G.B.之间不存在任何形式的合同关系。

法庭的判决基于三个要点:

1. C.E.G.B.在1989年文件中采用的语言;
2. 文件的操作方式;
3. 双方如何理解文件的证据。

根据事实,法庭确信,由于缺乏相互义务,双方之间不存在任何雇佣合同,因为公司没有义务提供工作,申请人也没有义务在被提供工作时从事工作。两位申请人对这一判决提出上诉,该事项被提交至上诉法院。

The court of appeal decision:

Ward LJ in the appeal court held that the only evidence which is relevant to the decision of the case was the 1989 documentation and the actual operation of the documentation, including the intention of the parties was not material to the case. He contended that while the first instance judges were correct in stating that the 1989documentation imposed no obligation on the respondent company to provide work, it did, however, impose obligations when such needs for work arose, the applicants were required to meet and perform the relevant services of a tour guide. Ward LJ interpreted there to exist an obligation by the company to provide a *"reasonable share of work...whenever the company had work available"* and an obligation by the applicants to *"take a reasonable amount of work once they have agreed to act as guides for the company."*

Chadwick LJ agreed with Ward LJ's approach that solely focused on the wording of the 1989 document. He argued that the words, *"as required"* were a clear indication that the applicants had duties to perform when they were needed. The court of appeal reached a unanimous decision to allow the appeal by the applicants and hold that they were under contracts of employment by the C.E.G.B.. The matter was again appealed by the respondent company, and it was delivered to the House of Lords for further consideration.

上诉法院判决：

上诉法院的沃德大法官认为，唯一与本案判决有关的证据是 1989 年文件，而文件的实际操作，包括当事人的意图，对本案并不重要。他认为，虽然一审法官认定 1989 年文件没有规定被告公司提供工作的义务是正确的，但是它确实规定了在出现工作需要时的义务，申请人必须满足做导游的要求并提供相关服务。沃德大法官解释，公司有义务提供“**合理的工作份额……只要公司有工作需要时**”，申请人有义务“**一旦同意担任公司的导游，就应承担合理的工作量**”。

查德威克大法官同意沃德大法官只关注 1989 年文件措辞的做法。他认为，“**按要求**”这几个字清楚地表明，申请人有义务在被需要时履行职责。上诉法院达成一致决定，支持申请人提出的上诉，并判定她们是 C.E.G.B. 的雇佣合同下的雇员。该事项再次经被申请人公司上诉，并被提交至上议院进一步审议。

The House of Lords decision:

Lord Irvine began his judgment by a detailed account of the Court of Appeal decision and stated that it was in his opinion incorrect to focus solely on the words in the 1989 documentation, which stated *"casual as required"*. He submitted that while it may be correct in many circumstances to focus on the wording in the employment documentation, this can only be so when the circumstance allows: *"In my judgment it would only be appropriate to determine the issue in these cases solely by reference to the documents in March 1989, if it appeared from their own terms and/ or from what the parties said or did then, or subsequently, that they intended them to constitute an exclusive memorial of their relationship."*

Lord Irvine continued to state that the approach by the first instance court, which focused also on the reality of interaction between the parties, were to be favoured. He thought that the intentions of the parties were crucial, which was displayed by what the parties said and did, starting from 1989. An example, as Lord Irvine suggested which was material to the case, that during 1994, Mrs Carmichael was not available to work when there was work provided on 17 occasions, and Mrs Lesse on eight. They were not punished for disciplinary reasons; this led the court to believe that the decision on whether or not to undertake work was purely in control of the applicants. The court also based parts of its decision on a sentence in Mrs Carmichael's application form, which

上议院判决：

欧文大法官在开始作出判决时详细叙述了上诉法院的裁决，并指出，他认为只关注1989年文件中的措辞“临时按需”是不正确的。他提出，虽然在许多情况下侧重于雇佣文件中的措辞可能是正确的，但是只有在情况允许时，才可这样做：“根据我的判断，只有当从文件自身的条款和/或双方当时或后来的言行来看，或其后打算将这些文件作为双方之间关系的唯一记录，才可以仅通过参考1989年3月的文件来确定这些案件中的问题。”

欧文大法官继续指出，一审法院的做法侧重于当事方之间互动的现实，这种做法是可取的。他认为，1989年以来各方的言行所表明的各方的意图至关重要。正如欧文大法官所举的一个例子，对本案具有重大意义，1994年，卡迈克尔夫人有17次在被提供工作时无法工作，莱斯夫人有8次。她们没有受到纪律处分；这使法院认为，关于是否从事工作的决定完全由两位申请人控制。法院的部分判决中还基于卡迈克尔夫人申请表中的一句话，其中指出“兼职临时安排最适合我的个人情况！”最终，正如欧文大法官所言，双方之间只存在某种道德义务感，而没有任何法律义务。

stated "the part-time casual arrangement would suit my personal circumstances ideally!" Ultimately, as Lord Irvine suggested, there existed only some sense of moral obligation between the parties instead of anything legal.

Lord Irvine ended his judgment by stating that even if the decision is to be solely based on the 1989 documentation, the outcome would be no different. He stated that *"casual as required"* imposed no obligation on either parties and no contracts were created in the process, that *"the documents did no more than provide a framework for a series of successive ad hoc contracts of service or for services which the parties might subsequently make."*

Lord Hoffman:

After agreeing with Lord Irvine's judgment, Lord Hoffman presented another vital judgment as to how future employment status cases are to be treated. He did so by suggesting the *"question of fact and question of law."*

It was Lord Hoffman's opinion that in such cases there are always a distinction between questions of fact and law, that the formation of documents and the details of the parties' interaction are almost always a question of fact. He argued that the Court of Appeal was wrong to treat the 1989 documentation as a legal document paralleled to actual contracts, the two judges, Ward and Chadwick LJ incorrectly labelled the document as a question of law. Lord Hoffman explained that the reason for the document being

欧文大法官在结束其判词时说明，即使决定完全基于 1989 年文件，结果也不会有什么不同。他认为，“临时按需”不要求任何一方承担任何义务，在这一过程中也没有订立任何合同，“这些文件只不过是为一系列连续的临时服务合同或当事人随后可能提供的服务提供了一个框架”。

霍夫曼大法官：

霍夫曼大法官在同意欧文大法官的判词之后，提出了关于如何处理未来雇佣身份案件的另一个重要判决，即“事实问题和法律问题”。

霍夫曼大法官认为，在这种情况下，事实问题和法律问题总是有区别的，文件的形成和双方当事人之间互动细节几乎均是事实问题。他认为，上诉法院将 1989 年文件视为与实际合同平等地位的法律文件是错误的，沃德和查德威克两位大法官错误地将该文件标示为法律问题。霍夫曼大法官解释说，该文件之所以是事实问题，是因为“这些信件不是由律师起草的，其语言极其简洁。要将其理解为一份完整的书面合同，上诉法院不得不解释其中的‘基于临时按需’这一晦涩的短语，作为

under a question of fact is because *"the letters were not drafted by a lawyer and their language was extremely concise. To construe them as a complete written contract left the Court of Appeal having to interpret the cryptic phrase 'on a casual as required basis' in what they, as judges, took to be its natural and ordinary meaning, without the assistance of the evidence of what the parties had understood or how the contract had been operated."*

The distinction between the questions of fact and law also required the court to look at both the contracts or documents and the actual interactions between the parties since it was in the Lords' opinion that similar cases would always involve within them a mix of law and facts.

Ultimately, the House of Lords reached a unanimous decision that the appeal made by the respondent company is to be allowed and the original decision by the Industrial Tribunal is to be reinstated.

Comments

The essence of the present judgment rests on the House of Lords' wise decision on which elements to focus on when dealing with employment status disputes. Its decision to not regard written documents as the primary authority and to separate the questions of fact and law renders this case a valuable precedent for future cases.

However, the House of Lords' decision to move away from solely focusing on documents and to investigate the reality may,

法官，在没有证据证明当事人是何种理解或合同是如何运作的情况下，应将其理解为其字面意义”。

事实和法律问题的区别还要求法院同时审查合同或文件以及当事人之间的实际互动，因为大法官们认为，类似的案件总是法律和事实的混合。

最后，上议院一致决定支持被申请人公司的上诉，恢复劳资争议法庭的原始判决。

案件评述

本判决的实质在于上议院在处理雇佣身份争议时明智地决定关注哪些要素。上议院不将书面文件视为主要权威，并将事实问题与法律问题分开的决定，使本案成为今后案件的宝贵先例。

然而，上议院不再只关注文件并调查现实情况的决定今后可能对临时工更有利。例如，如果雇主有意起草文件，将某些

in the future, be more beneficial to casual workers. For instance, where employers purposefully draft documents to categorize certain employees as "casual workers", but in reality the employees worked full-time and believed themselves to be full-time employees, the courts may be encouraged to look past the documents and declare them employees.

雇员归类为“临时工”，但实际上这些雇员是全职工作并认为自己是全职雇员，则法院可能愿意忽视这些文件，并宣布他们为正式雇员。

Case 2 Lane v Shire Roofing Co (Oxford) Ltd

—Employment status and breach of the duty of care

Preface:

I can imagine, as any reader of such subject would feel, a sense of boredom, stress, or an inevitable emotion to regard parts of the previous articles as works of mundane legal literature. It is a rare occasion indeed that the description of the facts of the following case including its subject, dare I say, demonstrates the resemblance of the opening of a mystery novel. I have done so in hopes of lifting your spirit while reading, please read the following facts carefully, and bear in mind that this case deals with employment status and the breach of the duty of care by the employer.

Facts

Mr Lane arrived early that day, as it was his first day on a new contract. He had worked as a carpenter for many years now, specializing in roof building and such. The work for that day involved the retiling of the porch roof of a house owned by

案例 2　莱恩诉夏尔屋顶（牛津）有限公司案
——雇佣身份与雇主违反注意义务

引言:

我能够想象，正如任何一位此类主题的读者会感受到的那样，一种无聊和略有压力的感觉，或不可避免地将前几篇的部分内容视为单调的法律作品。但是我敢断言，下述案件事实（包括其主题）的描述，非常像一部推理小说的开始，这确实是一个罕见的情形。我这样做是为了提振你阅读时的精神，请仔细阅读以下事实并记住本案涉及雇佣身份和雇主违反注意义务的行为。

案件事实

莱恩先生那一天到得很早，因为这是他新工作的第一天。他做了很多年的木匠，专门从事屋顶建筑之类的工作。那天的工作是重新装修伯德夫妇房子的门廊屋顶，对莱恩先生来说幸运的是，两位业主都有各自的事情，这使他可以静下心，整个

Mr and Mrs Bird, and luckily for Mr Lane, both the owners were otherwise occupied, leaving him at peace, working alone in their property that entire morning. Just before Mrs Bird left the house, she saw that the ladder had already been put against the wall, the tools taken out of the toolbox and a few cut slates laying around. She was satisfied that Mr Lane had already begun working.

After the Birds left, Mr Lane thought to himself that the first thing on his list today was the cutting of a few slates on the roof. All seemed to be going well at first, the procedures were followed, slates were being cut at a relatively consistent pace, it would seem like so to anyone that Mr and Mrs Bird would return home later to find their roof finely cut, and everything working perfectly...

Later that day, Mrs Bird just finished whatever was occupying her that entire morning, and she returned home quickly after.

The first thing she saw, was that the ladder had been folded and collected, so were the tools, the dust left around by the cutting of the slates had also been cleaned, all that was missing, was Mr Lane. As Mrs Bird approached the house to find a considerable amount of blood on the concrete surface next to the front door, worried, she quickly goes to locate Mr Lane. Few moments later, Mrs Bird found Mr Lane sitting in his car, though he looked strange, in a sense, much differently when compared with the morning.

Mr Lane was obviously injured, a small amount of blood was leaking from his ears, his eyes were wide open, yet from his facial expression it was as if he was blind. Mrs Bird tried to talk to him, though all Mr Lane uttered was he needed aspirin and wished to go

上午独自在他们的房子里工作。在伯德夫人离开家之前，她看到梯子已经靠在墙上，工具也从工具箱里拿了出来，周围放着几块切割过的石板瓦。她对莱恩先生已经开始工作感到满意。

伯德夫妇离开后，莱恩先生心想，今天的第一件事就是在屋顶上切割下几块石板瓦。起初一切似乎顺利，遵守程序，石板瓦的切割速度相对一致，任何人都会认为，伯德夫妇稍后回家时会发现他们的屋顶被精细切割，一切将完美进展……

那天晚些时候，伯德夫人刚刚结束了整个上午的工作，很快就回家了。

首先映入她眼帘的是，梯子和工具都被折叠并收集起来了，石板瓦切割留下的灰尘也被清理干净，唯有莱恩先生不知所踪。当伯德夫人走近房子时，发现前门旁边的混凝土表面上有大量的血迹，这使她很担心，于是迅速动身去寻找莱恩先生。几分钟后，伯德夫人发现莱恩先生坐在他的车里，但是从某种意义上说，他看起来很奇怪，与那天早上相比，判若两人。

莱恩先生显然受伤了，耳朵里有少量血迹，双目圆睁，但他呆滞的面部表情使他看起来更像一个盲人。伯德夫人试着和他说话，尽管莱恩先生只说他需要阿司匹林，并且想回家。令伯德夫人惊讶的是，当被问及是否需要看医生时，他

home. To Mrs Bird's surprise, when asked whether he needed to see the doctors, he quickly declined.

As any ordinary, friendly citizen would, Mrs Bird took him to the hospital, where he was diagnosed to have suffered trauma on his head, causing serious brain damage. Mr Lane was unable to recall any events which might have led to his injury, since he was working alone that morning, no one would be able to know what had happened.

It would appear reasonable to ask why was Mr Lane there that morning? Despite the obvious answer of carpenter work, it would be useful to know that Mr Lane was working for a job provided by Mr Whittaker, the proprietor of Shire Roofing Co. Prior to meeting with Mr Whittaker, Mr Lane worked as a one-man firm, obtaining self-employed fiscal status, with a right to the 714 tax exemption certificates, which was only available for self-employed individuals. Though the workload began to unwillingly reduce, leaving Mr Lane with no choice but to respond to an advertisement posted by Mr Whittaker, which intended to recruit carpenters. Mr Lane was subsequently employed and Mr Whittaker provided him one job, which was almost over when Mr Lane accepted, per Mr Whittaker's request the second job, taking place at the Birds estate.

Looking back at the accident, there were two mysteries that would boggle the brightest of minds. How were the ladders and tools so organized if Mr Lane suffered so severe of an injury which made him lose part of his memory? And how was there so much blood near the door when Mr Lane was only bleeding a significant

很快拒绝了。

如同任何一位普通而友好的公民，伯德夫人把他送到了医院，在那里他被诊断为头部受伤，导致严重的脑损伤。莱恩先生无法回忆起任何可能导致他受伤的事件。那天早上他独自工作，没有人能知道究竟发生了什么。

一个合理的问题是，莱恩先生那天早上为什么在那里？尽管木匠工作是显而易见的答案，但应获知的有用信息是，莱恩先生是在做一份夏尔屋顶公司的老板惠特克先生提供的工作。在与惠特克先生会面之前，莱恩先生独自工作，获得了自雇的财税身份，有权获得714免税证书，这也只适用于个体经营者。但是无可奈何的是，业务量开始减少，莱恩先生别无选择，只能回应惠特克先生发布的一则招聘木匠的广告。莱恩先生随后被雇佣，惠特克先生为他提供了一单工作，当莱恩先生按照惠特克先生的要求接受了在伯德住宅的第二单工作时，第一单的工作几乎已经结束了。

回顾这起事故，有两个谜团会让就算最聪明的人都感到困惑。如果莱恩先生受了如此严重的伤，失去了部分记忆，梯子和工具是如何妥当收起来的？当莱恩先生只从耳朵里流了少量的血时，门附近又怎么会有这么多血？这些问题可能永远无法获得答案，但其存在一些需要回答的法律问题。

smaller amount of blood from his ears? These questions may never be answered, yet there existed legal problems in need of answering.

Mr Lane, now as the plaintiff, claimed for damages for his injuries suffered while working as a result of an absence of the duty of care. Shire Roofing Co as the defendant argues that Mr Lane was not an employee, but instead an independent contractor who was employed on a contract-by-contract basis.

Issue

1. What is the standard for recognizing employees employed on a contract-by-contract basis?

2. What duties of care are owed by the employer to his/her employees?

Judicial View

The first instance decision:

The first instance judges laid out the relevant facts and took a guess out of common sense on what might have occurred that day, *"I find that the injuries that he did suffer were caused by that fall from that ladder. On the balance of probabilities I find that that fall was due to a sudden loss of balance by the plaintiff himself, presumably due to a momentary lack of attention."* The judge ignored much of the details of the facts, though it was enough to deduce from

莱恩先生现在是原告，他主张雇主缺乏注意义务而使其在工作中受伤，并要求赔偿损失。夏尔屋顶公司作为被告辩称，莱恩先生不是一名雇员，而是一名独立缔约人，根据每一单工作单独受聘。

争议焦点

1. 根据每一单聘用的雇员的身份确认标准是什么？

2. 雇主对雇员负有什么注意义务？

司法观点

一审法院的判决：

一审法官列举了相关事实，并根据常识猜测了当天可能发生的情况，“我认为他受到的伤是从那个梯子上摔下所造成的。从概率上看，我认为那是由于原告自己突然失去平衡，大概是由于一时注意力不足”。法官忽略了事实的许多细节，但是根据常识足够推断，上述描述的很可能是当时所发生的事情。

common sense that the description above was quite possibly what had occurred.

With the facts established, the judge went on to analyse the advantages that both parties would enjoy if Mr Lane was hired as an independent contractor. The judge argued that as the world develops more flexibility would be offered to employment positions, that since the defendant company is a rather newly established operation, it would be of advantage for them to *"enter into contracts for specific works without having a continuous payroll."* It would also make more sense for Mr Lane to work as an independent contractor since he had always worked independently in the past and would be subject to more favourable tax provisions had he continued doing so. The judge continued to state that *"the plaintiff was obviously capable of working without supervision and that Mr Whittaker relied upon him to do so."*

Furthermore, it was stated in the facts that there was no indication nor guarantee that Mr Whittaker would provide Mr Lane further contracts upon finishing the current two. Ultimately, the first instance judge submitted that the plaintiff was held to be an independent contractor the whole time he was working for the defendant company and because of this there was owed no duty of care by the defendant. He further stated that even if there were any duties owed, there would be no breach since it would reasonably be safe enough to conduct the job via a ladder. Mr Lane had since appealed against both parts of the decision.

在确定事实之后，法官接着分析了如果莱恩先生被聘为独立缔约人双方将享有的好处。法官认为，世界的发展将为雇用职位提供更大的灵活性，由于被告公司是一家新成立经营的公司，因此他们“**在不需要连续付工资的情况下，为特定工作而签订合同**”将是有利的。莱恩先生作为独立缔约人而工作也更合理，因为他过去一直独立工作，如果他继续这样做，将获得更优惠的税收待遇。法官继续论述，“**原告显然能够在没有监督的情况下工作，惠特克先生信赖他能这样做**”。

此外，事实表明，没有迹象或保证惠特克先生会在目前两单工作完成后向莱恩先生提供更多工作。最终，一审法官认为，原告在为被告公司工作的整个期间均是一个独立缔约人，因此被告不负有雇主的注意义务。他还认为，即使存在任何义务，也不会有违反的情形，因为使用梯子进行工作是相当安全的。莱恩先生对判决的上述两部分均提出了上诉。

Court of Appeal:

Henry LJ first concurred with the inference that the first instance judge drew from the facts, and stated, *"the judge... making reasonable deductions from the known facts, and sensibly refusing tobe nudged off course by mere possibilities for which there was no evidence."* Though he quickly began to disagree with the trial judge, as he introduced two tests on employment status.

Control test and economic reality test:

Henry LJ thought that the below question had to be asked to satisfy the control test: *"who lays down what is to be done, the way in which it is to be done, the means by which it is to be done, and the time when it is done? Who provides (i.e. hires and fires) the team by which it is done, and who provides the material, plant and machinery and tools used?"* It was obvious that the defendant company would be the answer to most of these questions, except that Mr Lane used his own equipment for the job. Henry LJ soon realized the unsatisfactory nature of the control test, since in cases of skilled employees, it would be unnecessary for the employer to exercise control over their work, but that does not indicate that there exists no employment relationship between the parties. To understand the full picture, Henry LJ began his analysis on the second test, which focused on asking, *"whose business was it: was the workman carrying on his own business, or was he carrying on*

上诉法院：

亨利大法官首先同意了一审法官从事实中得出的推论，并指出，“法官……从已知的事实中做出合理的推论，明智地拒绝了被没有证据的可能性推离轨道”。但是他很快就开始不同意一审法官的观点，并引入了两项关于雇佣身份的验证标准。

控制验证标准和经济现实验证标准：

亨利大法官认为，为了满足控制验证标准，必须提出以下问题：“谁制定了要做的事情、方式、手段以及时间？谁提供（即雇用和解雇）完成此项工作的团队，谁提供所用的材料、设备、机械和工具？”很明显，除了莱恩先生使用自己的设备进行工作外，其他绝大部分问题的答案均是被告公司。亨利大法官很快意识到控制验证标准令人不满意的性质，因为对于熟练雇员来说，雇主没有必要对他们的工作进行控制，但这并不表明双方之间不存在雇佣关系。为了解事件全貌，亨利大法官开始对第二个验证标准进行分析，重点是问：“这是谁的生意：工人是在经营自己的生意，还是在经营雇主的生意？”这就是著名的“经济现实”验证标准。

that of his employers?" This was the famous "economic reality" test.

Upon applying the economic reality test, Henry LJ stated that the building contract in question was entered into not by Mr Lane, but between Mr Whittaker and The Birds, for an agreed price of 389 pounds. Mr Whittaker subsequently agreed to pay Mr Lane 200 pounds for the job. Henry LJ argued that in these situations it was important to ask whose business this was, as he laid out two possible scenarios for two separate answers.

1. An employer engages men "on the lump" to perform labour, and in this situation the men are clearly employees.

2. An employer employs a specialist contractor to perform a part of a general contract, in this situation the specialist would be an independent contractor.

It was in Henry LJ's opinion that the plaintiff Mr Lane rests somewhere in between the two scenarios, yet is significantly closer to the former. Finally, Henry LJ stated, *"it was the respondents' business and not the appellant's. In my judgment, therefore, they owed the duties of employers to the appellant."*

Duty of care:

The next question facing Henry LJ is whether the defendant company owed a duty of care to Mr Lane. Mr Lane relied on regulation 7 of the Construction (Working Places) Regulations 1966 that stated the equipment used for the job must be "appropriate" and *"sufficient and suitable for the purpose."* The plaintiff sought

在应用经济现实验证标准时，亨利大法官表示，本案的建筑合同不是由莱恩先生签订的，而是惠特克先生和伯德夫妇之间以 389 英镑商定的价格签订的。惠特克先生随后同意为此单工作，并付给莱恩先生 200 英镑的报酬。亨利大法官认为，在这些情况下，重要的是要询问这是谁的生意，他为两个不同的答案列出了两种可能的情况。

1. 雇主雇用“一笔付清”的人从事劳动，该等情况下，这些人显然是雇员。

2. 雇主雇用专业承包商履行总合同的一部分，该等情况下，专业承包商应为独立缔约人。

亨利大法官认为，原告莱恩先生介于两种情况之间，但明显更接近前者。最后，亨利大法官说，“这是被上诉人的生意，而不是上诉人的。因此，在我看来，他们对上诉人负有雇主的责任”。

注意义务：

亨利大法官面临的下一个问题是，被告公司是否对莱恩先生负有注意义务。莱恩先生依据《1966 年施工（工作场所）条例》第 7 条规定，即用于施工作业的设备必须“适当”且“足够且适合于该目的”。原告利用这一规定来主张，他用于工作的那个梯子不适当且不适合其目的，这意味着他的雇主违反了

to use this regulation to argue that the ladder which he used for the work was neither appropriate nor suitable for the purpose, meaning his employer was in breach of the duty of care.

The first instance judge's reasons for arguing the contrary were that he thought it would be enough to focus solely on the side of the house which the plaintiff fell from his ladder and ignore the other two slopes of the roof, the side which Mr Lane fell from was relatively safe for any work to be conducted. Henry LJ thought otherwise, he first stated that the diction of regulation 7 called for an analysis on the foreseeability of risk, meaning that if it was foreseeable that Mr Lane would injure himself with a ladder, then the defendant company would be in breach of the duty of care. Henry LJ gathered the facts on the appearance of the building and stated that *"For my part, on the primary facts as found by the trial judge, I would have found that it was not appropriate to use a ladder... because overreaching and/or some other loss of balance was foreseeable, as the facts of so many cases before these courts show. So I would find for the plaintiff on the question of liability."* Henry LJ continued to argue that it was also incorrect on the part of the trial judge to ignore the other two slopes, since the work in question was likely to continue for another day or two, meaning the possibility that Mr Lane would eventually use the other two slopes of the house.

Ultimately, the Court of Appeal declared the following judgment, *"Order, Appeal allowed with costs; judgment entered for*

注意义务。

一审法官提出不同论点的理由是，他认为，仅关注原告从梯子上摔下来的房屋那一侧就足够了，而忽略了屋顶的另外两个斜坡，莱恩先生从上面摔下来的那一侧对于进行任何工作来说都是相对安全的。亨利大法官则不这么认为，他首先指出，第7条的措辞要求对风险的可预见性进行分析，这意味着如果可以预见莱恩先生会在梯子上受伤，那么被告公司将违反注意义务。亨利大法官收集了建筑物外观的事实，并说明“就我而言，根据一审法官发现的主要事实，我认为使用梯子是不适当的……因为正如这些法院审理的许多案件的事实所表明的那样，胳膊的过度伸展和/或其他一些失衡是可以预见的。因此，我会在赔偿责任问题上偏向原告作出判决”。亨利大法官继续分析，一审法官忽视另外两个斜坡也是不正确的，因为这单工作可能再继续一两天，这意味着莱恩先生最终可能使用房子的另外两个斜坡。

最后，上诉法院宣布了以下判决：“判令，上诉及其费用获得支持；判决金额为102,500英镑，加上1993年5月26日判

the sum of £102,500 plus interest at the judgment rate from May 26, 1993; legal aid taxation of the plaintiff's costs; leave to appeal to the House of Lords refused."

Comments

While it is truly an almost unbearably unfortunate reality that one may never uncover what had truly occurred that day in the Birds' property, the Court of Appeal did provide an insightful judgment that was cited numerous times in later cases when deciding employment status and the duty of care. Especially, one must remember the "economic reality test", which is still regarded today as one of the leading tests on employment status. I would suggest going back to the last article and combine all the tests explained by the courts in the two cases, which would certainly provide much insights on understanding how employment status cases are treated in the UK.

决利率的利息；对原告费用的法律援助征税；不得向上议院提出上诉。”

案件评述

虽然，一个几乎令人无法忍受的不幸现实是，人们可能永远无法发现当天在伯德住宅中发生的真实情况，但上诉法院确实提供了一项富有见地的判决，在后来的案件中，在决定雇佣身份和雇主的注意义务时，多次援引了本案的判决。特别是，我们必须记住“经济现实验证标准”，它至今仍被视为雇佣身份的主要验证标准之一。我建议回到上一篇文章，并结合两个法院在这两个案例中所解释的所有验证标准，这必会对理解雇佣身份案件在英国如何处理提供很多见解。

Case 3 Uber BV v Aslam

—Are Uber drivers workers?

Preface:

With the world progressing economically and technologically, jobs of all kinds are being created. This may be beneficial for the overall public searching for employment opportunities, though it has created an extra level of uncertainty in the legal field concerning employment status and the definition of employment and work. The current case focuses on the relationship between "Uber", a car hiring company similar to "DiDi" in China, and the drivers using Uber's services. It was a questionable fact of law whether the drivers using the Uber App to pick up passengers should be considered as "workers" under the Employment Rights Act 1996 ("the Act").

"Workers" in English law is distinct from "employees", as they do not have all the legal rights of an employee. Though in this case and many others in the past or future, it is crucial to determine whether one can be in law considered a "worker" mainly due to these two reasons:

1. Workers are protected under the national minimum wage regulations.

案例 3　优步公司诉阿斯拉姆案
——优步司机是工人吗?

引言:

随着世界经济和技术的进步，各类工作机会正在被创造。这可能有利于公众寻找就业机会，但是这在雇佣身份以及就业和工作定义的法律领域造成了额外的不确定性。本案聚焦“优步”，一家类似于中国“滴滴”的汽车雇佣公司和使用其服务的司机之间的关系。一个需要商榷的法律事实为，使用优步应用程序接送乘客的司机是否应被视为《1996 年就业权利法》项下的“工人”。

英国法律中的“工人”与“雇员”不同，因为他们不具有雇员拥有的所有法律权利 。但是在本案以及在过去或将来的许多其他案例中，确定一个人是否可以在法律上被视为“工人”是至关重要的，主要是由于以下两个原因:

1. 工人受国家最低工资规定的保护。

2. Workers are entitled to paid annual leave.

The facts of the current case are unfortunately dense and complicated, formatted differently from the past cases, as there is no clear line of events that occurred, instead it is only necessary to explain the nature of the relationship between Uber and its Drivers.

Facts

The first respondent is Uber BV, a Dutch company that owns the right to the design and services provided by the Uber App. The second respondent is Uber London Ltd (Uber London), a subsidiary of Uber BV which operates in London, UK. The third respondent is Uber Britannia Ltd, another subsidiary which operates outside of London. In the below analysis and explanations, when applicable, all three respondents will be referred to together as "Uber".

The claimants are a group of individuals who work or had worked for Uber as drivers for private hiring. The drivers claimed to berecognized in law as workers and to enjoy the relevant rights and benefits. For the purpose of clarity, the court has limited its consideration on two main claimants, Mr Aslam and Mr Farrar.

The Uber App operates in a way where the driver who logs in his account would usually receive a notification of a requested trip, he would be told first the passenger's name and his/her rating, and have 10 seconds to decide whether to accept the current request. The driver and passenger are subsequently put in direct contact though neither has the other person's mobile number for privacy reasons. As the trip is

2. 工人享有带薪年假。

不幸的是，当前案件的事实错综复杂，且因为没有明确的事件发生，所以形式与过去的案件不同，我们只需要解释优步与其司机之间关系的性质。

案件事实

第一个被申请人是优步公司，这家荷兰公司拥有优步应用程序的设计和其所提供服务的权利。第二个被申请人是优步伦敦有限公司（以下简称伦敦优步），该公司是优步公司在英国伦敦运营的子公司。第三个被申请人是优步大不列颠有限公司，这是另一家在伦敦以外地区运营的子公司。在以下分析和解释中，如果适用，所有 3 个被申请人将被统称为“优步”。

申请人是一群在优步或曾经在优步做过私人雇佣司机的个人群体。司机的诉求为在法律上被认定为工人而拥有相关的权益。为清晰起见，法院将审议范围限制在两个主要申请人身上，即阿斯拉姆先生和法拉尔先生。

优步应用程序的运行方式是，登录其账户的司机通常会收到请求行程的通知，他会首先被告知乘客的姓名和评分，并有 10 秒钟的时间来决定是否接受当前请求。司机和乘客随后会进行直接联系，但是出于隐私原因他们均没有对方的移动电话号码。当行程完成并到达目的地时，司机能够在应用程序上完成行程，票价将自动计算。

completed and the destination reached, the driver is able to complete the trip on the App, the fare would be calculated automatically.

Uber BV pays the drivers a weekly amount based on the number of trip each driver had completed. A service fee would be deducted and retained by Uber BV. For the two claimants in this case, the service fee was 20%.

Uber has the power to prohibit drivers from contacting the passenger, or vice versa after the trip is completed unless any properties had been left in the car. Uber also utilizes a rating system where the drivers would be subject to warnings and be eventually logged off the app when the rating becomes too low or the driver has declined too many requests consecutively.

The drivers must possess and use his own vehicle and pay for any charges made while working by the vehicle, such as fuel, insurance or any road tax. The vehicle must also be in good condition and subject to a limit on the number of years driven.

The drivers are expected to follow the guidelines provided by Uber on how to or not to act while working. For instance, every driver was told the following, *"We continually look at your driver rating, client comments, and feedback provided to us. Maintaining a high rating overall helps keep a top tier service to riders. Going on duty means you are willing and able to accept trip requests. Rejecting too many requests leads to rider confusion about availability. You should be off duty if not able to take requests."* Uber also has the power to decide whether to refund the passenger the fare when complaints are received for certain drivers.

优步公司每周根据每个司机完成的行程数量向司机支付金额。优步公司将扣除并保留服务费。本案中，两名申请人被扣的服务费为20%。

优步有权禁止司机和乘客在行程结束后相互联系，除非车内有任何财物遗失。优步还运用了一个评级系统，在该系统中，当评级变低或司机连续拒绝太多请求时，司机将受到警告，并最终被在应用程序中注销。

司机必须拥有和使用自己的车辆，并支付车辆工作期间产生的任何费用，如燃油、保险或任何道路税。车辆必须处于良好状态，并受到驾驶年限的限制。

司机们须遵循优步提供的关于工作时如何行动或不行动的指导方针。例如，每个司机均被告知，“我们会不断查看您的驾驶员评分、客户评论和向我们提供的反馈。保持高评分有助于为乘客提供一流的服务。上岗意味着您愿意并能够接受行程请求。拒绝太多请求会导致乘客对司机可用性的困惑。您如果不能接受请求，就不应该上班”。优步也有权在收到某些对司机的投诉时，决定是否向乘客退还车费。

Every driver was asked to sign a "partner registration form" which states that they were bound and must comply with the relevant terms and conditions. Starting from 2015, the drivers were also told to sign a Service Agreement which states that a legal agreement was to be made between Uber BV and "Customer", a word used to describe *"an independent company in the business of providing transportation services."* The purpose of such agreement is to state that Uber BV provides no transportation service in any form, but only provides the service on the app to form agreements between the drivers (customers) and the passengers (users). It was stated in the agreement that it *"creates a legal and direct business relationship between customer and the user, to which neither Uber [BV] nor any of its affiliates in the territory is a party."*

Uber also set written terms and conditions between it and the passengers, who are required to accept the terms before logging into the app. The agreement states that *"Uber UK accepts PHV Bookings acting as disclosed agent for the Transportation Provider (as principal)... For the avoidance of doubt: Uber UK does not itself provide transportation services, and is not a Transportation Provider. Uber UK acts as intermediary between you and the Transportation Provider."* It is obvious here that Uber is trying to identify themselves as a mere booking agent.

Issue

When are individuals working under the gig economy, and

每个司机均被要求签署一份“合作伙伴登记表”，声明他们受到约束，必须遵守相关条款和条件。从2015年开始，司机们还被告知要签署一份服务协议，该协议规定优步公司与“客户”之间将签订一份法律协议，“客户”一词用于描述“一家从事运输服务的独立公司”。该协议的目的是声明优步公司不提供任何形式的交通服务，而仅提供应用程序上的服务，以形成司机（客户）和乘客（用户）之间的协议。协议中指出，其“在客户和用户之间建立了一种法律和直接的业务关系，优步公司或其在该地区的任何附属公司均不是该业务关系的一方”。

优步另制定了他们和乘客之间的书面条款，乘客必须在登录应用程序之前接受这些条款。该协议规定，“英国优步接受私人车辆租赁预订，作为交通服务提供商（当事人）的明确代理人……为免生疑问：英国优步本身不提供交通服务，也不是交通服务提供商。英国优步作为您和交通服务提供商之间的中介”。很明显，优步试图将自己定位为一个单纯的预订代理机构。

争议焦点

在零工经济下工作的个人，特别是优步司机，何种情况下

specifically Uber drivers, considered workers?

Judicial View

Section 230(3) on "workers" in the Act defines a worker in the following way:

"In this Act 'worker'... means an individual who has entered into or works under... (a) a contract of employment, or (b) any other contract... whereby the individual undertakes to perform personally any work or services for another party to the contract whose status is not by virtue of the contract that of a client or customer of any profession or business undertaking carried on by the individual..."

The first instance decision:

The employment tribunal heard this case during 2016 and decided that the claimants were indeed "workers" for the definition under the Act, specifically within the meaning of limb (b). The tribunal held that the claimants were workers for Uber London when they (a) had the app turned on, (b) was within the overall location where they were authorized and (c) were accepting trips.

Uber has since appealed and when the case reached the Employment Appeal Tribunal, the appeal was dismissed, and Uber appealed again to the Supreme Court.

被视为工人?

司法观点

《1996年就业权利法》关于“工人”的第230（3）条对工人的定义如下：

> 在该法中，“工人”……是指一个已经根据以下情形签署合同或工作的个人……（a）雇佣合同，或（b）任何其他合同……根据该合同，该个人承诺亲自为合同的另一方履行任何工作或服务，而该另一方的身份不是（根据该合同）属于该个人从事的任何专业或业务的客户或顾客……

一审法院判决：

就业法庭在2016年审理了这一案件，并判定申请人确实是该法定义的“工人”，特别是在（b）款的含义范围内。法庭认为，申请人在以下情形下是伦敦优步的工人：（a）打开了应用程序；（b）在他们获得授权的整个区域内；（c）正在接受行程订单。

优步此后提出上诉，当案件提交就业上诉法庭时被驳回，优步再次向最高法院提出上诉。

The Supreme Court decision:

Uber relied on the following points for their arguments in this case:

1. According to the above listed agreements, whenever a trip was accepted, a contract is created, but only between the passenger and the driver. Uber as an entity is no party to the contract and holds no responsibility for providing any transportation services.

2. Uber BV is in reality only a platform to act as a "payment collection agent" for the driver.

Lord Leggatt started by stating that the current case concerns only one critical issue: *"whether, for the purposes of the statutory definition, the claimants are to be regarded as working under contracts with Uber London."*

Lord Leggatt proceeded to analyse the facts in several different angles, to which formed an over complicated judgment, for the purpose of this article, I have since chosen only parts to discuss:

Uber London's authorization to act as amere booking agent:

Lord Leggatt pointed out that a crucial point which could lead to Uber's potential loss in the case is the fact that there exists no written agreement between Uber London and the drivers, which calls for the court's inference from the parties' conduct.

It is unlawful for any organization to operate a car hiring business or service without being licenced by Transport for London, the licensing authority. The only entity or party in this case which

最高法院判决：

优步在本案中就其主张所依据的论点如下：

1. 根据以上列出的协议，无论何时行程订单被接受，均会形成合同，但仅限于乘客和司机之间。优步作为一个实体不是合同的任何一方，不承担提供任何交通服务的责任。

2. 优步公司实际上只是一个平台，为司机充当“收款代理”。

莱加特大法官首先指出，目前的案件只涉及一个关键问题：“就法定定义而言，申请人是否应被视为与伦敦优步在合同下工作。”

莱加特大法官从几个不同的角度对事实进行了分析，从而形成了一个过于复杂的判决意见，出于本文目的，笔者只选择了部分进行讨论：

伦敦优步对于仅作为预订代理的授权问题：

莱加特大法官指出，可能导致优步在本案中败诉的一个关键点是，伦敦优步与司机之间没有书面协议，这就要求法院根据当事人的行为进行推断。

任何组织在未经伦敦交通局（许可机关）许可的情况下经营汽车租赁业务或服务是违法的。在本案中，唯一持有接受预订和提供车辆租赁服务许可证的实体或一方为伦敦优步。优步

holds the licence to accept bookings and provide vehicles hiring service is Uber London. Uber argued that it acting as an agent to aid the drivers in providing the service should comply with the licencing requirement. However, Lord Leggatt was not convinced by this, he stated that if Uber was to only act as an agent, both the driver and Uber would be viewed as accepting the booking while undertaking a contractual obligation owed to the passenger. If so, the driver would be violating the licencing agreement set out in s2(1) of the Private Hire Vehicles (London) Act 1998 for accepting private hiring contract without a valid licence. Lord Leggatt submitted that it is because of this point that he concluded *"the only contractual arrangement compatible with the licensing regime is one whereby Uber London as the licensed operator accepts private hire bookings as a principal (only) and, to fulfil its obligation to the passenger."*

Uber continued to assert that agency principles should in law be able to pass the licencing regime requirement. Though Lord Leggatt thought that this was unnecessary. Lord Leggatt stated that Uber's reliance on the terms which stated, *"acting as disclosed agent for the Transportation Provider"* is useless in the current context, due to the absence of any consent by the drivers to authorize Uber in becoming their agent. Lord Legatt further noted that one cannot merely create a contract between another and a third party by claiming to do so in a terms or condition document without proper authorization by that person to act as the principal. Lord Leggatt agreed with the employment tribunal's finding that the

辩称，其作为代理人协助司机提供服务符合许可证要求。然而，莱加特大法官对此并不信服，他表示，如果优步仅作为代理人，司机和优步均将被视为接受预订，同时承担对乘客的合同义务。如果是这样，司机将违反《1998 年私人租赁车辆（伦敦）法》第 2（1）条规定的许可协议，在没有有效许可证的情况下接受私人租赁合同。莱加特大法官认为，正是因为这一点，他得出结论：“**唯一与许可制度兼容的合同安排是，伦敦优步仅是作为当事人和许可运营商接受私人租赁预订，并履行其对乘客的义务。**”

优步继续辩称，代理原则在法律上应该能够通过许可制度的要求。但是莱加特大法官认为这是不必要的。莱加特大法官表示，优步对“**作为交通服务提供商的明确代理人**”条款的依赖在当前情况下是没有用的，因为司机没有同意授权优步成为他们的代理人。莱加特大法官进一步指出，一个人在没有该另一个人作为当事人的适当授权时不能仅仅通过在条款或条件文件中声称在另一个人和第三方之间订立合同。莱加特大法官同意就业法庭的裁决，即司机没有明显的行为授权伦敦优步作为代理人，唯一的依据是书面安排，而书面安排由于缺乏授权而变得无用。

莱加特大法官在结束对这一部分的判决意见时指出，“**一旦**

drivers did no apparent act to confer authority on Uber London to act as agent, that the only basis was the written arrangement, which becomes useless due to a lack of authority. Lord Leggatt concluded his judgment on this segment by stating, *"Once the assertion that Uber London contracts as a booking agent for drivers is rejected, the inevitable conclusion is that, by accepting a booking, Uber London contracts as principal with the passenger to carry out the booking."*

Protection of workers:

Lord Leggatt confirmed that the main purpose in employment cases which tread in the field of worker status is to protect the vulnerable workers from being paid too little or be forced to work excessively and other forms of unreasonable treatment. Lord Leggatt cited as tatement in *Byrne Bros (Formwork) Ltd v Baird [2002] I.C.R. 667*, *"The reason why employees are thought to need such protection is that they are in a subordinate and dependent position vis-à-vis their employers: the purpose of the Regulations is to extend protection to workers who are, substantively and economically, in the same position."* Using the subordination and protection argument, Lord Leggatt moved on to the difficult question on the definition of "worker". He proceeded to cite a plethora of case laws for the purpose of indicating that, for the purpose of the legislation and the protection of workers, it is never enough to simply regard one as a worker or not based on the written agreements or contracts. Lord Leggatt maintained that, *"It is the*

伦敦优步公司作为司机预订代理签订合同的说法被驳回，不可避免的结论是，通过接受预订，伦敦优步公司作为当事人与乘客签订合同而操作预订”。

对工人的保护：

莱加特大法官确认，在涉及工人身份领域的就业案件中，主要目的是保护弱势工人不受报酬过低或被迫过度工作以及其他形式的不合理待遇。莱加特大法官引用了拜恩兄弟有限公司诉贝尔德案（[2002] I.C.R.667）中的一项声明，“之所以认为雇员需要这种保护，是因为他们相对于雇主处于从属和依赖的地位：条例的目的是将保护扩大到在实质上和经济上处于同一地位的工人们”。利用从属关系和保护的论点，莱加特大法官继续讨论关于“工人”定义的困难问题。他接着列举了大量的案例，目的是表明，为了立法的目的和对工人的保护，仅仅以书面协议或合同为依据而将一个人视为或不视为工人是远远不够的。莱加特大法官坚称，“正是这样一个事实，即雇主往往能够规定此类合同条款，而从事工作的个人几乎没有或根本没有能力影响这些条款，他们才首先需要法律保护”。

very fact that an employer is often in a position to dictate such contract terms and that the individual performing the work has little or no ability to influence those terms that gives rise to the need for statutory protection in the first place."

One could understand that Lord Leggatt said so in order to prevent the employers from having too much power over workers. Applying this to the current case, the Supreme Court found that the Service Agreement mentioned above was indeed drafted by Uber's lawyers and presented to the drivers. Lord Leggatt questioned if any of the drivers actually read the agreement carefully since they must accept it if they wanted to use the Uber App.

The reality of the situation and the level of control:

As you may remember, my first article on English labour law was on the case *Carmichael v National Power Plc [1999] 1 W.L.R. 2042*, which stated that the courts should be encouraged to look at the reality of the facts and determine one's employment status. Lord Leggatt adopted this procedure and here were his findings:

1. The remuneration for the drivers is fixed by Uber and the drivers have no control over it.

2. The contractual terms which the drivers must follow and accept to perform their services are dictated by Uber.

3. While a certain level of freedom was given to the drivers on choosing when and where to work, their choices are often constrained by Uber.

4. The driver's rate of acceptance and cancellation of trip

我们可以理解，莱加特大法官这样说是为了防止雇主对工人拥有太大的权力。最高法院将这一点应用于本案，发现上述服务协议确实是优步的律师起草并提交给司机的。莱加特大法官质疑是否有司机真的仔细阅读了协议，因为如果他们想使用优步应用程序，就必须接受协议。

实际情况和控制水平：

您可能还记得，我的第一篇关于英国劳动法的文章是关于卡迈克尔诉国家电力公司案（[1999] 1 W.L.R.2042）。该案指出，应鼓励法院审视事实的真实性并确定一个人的雇佣身份。莱加特大法官采用了这一方法，他的调查结果如下：

1. 司机的报酬是由优步确定的，司机没有控制权。

2. 优步规定了司机执行服务必须遵守并接受的合同条款。

3. 虽然在选择工作时间和地点方面给予了司机一定程度的自由，但他们的选择往往受到优步的限制。

4. 司机对行程请求的接受率和取消率受到高度监视，如果

requests are highly monitored and would severely affect one's work if it reaches a certain limit.

5. Uber vets the types of car that may be used and dictates the route on all the trips.

6. The rating system which would result in warnings and termination of the driver's ability to use the app when it reaches a certain number.

7. Uber restricts communication between passengers and drivers to the minimum.

From the above reasons and an abundance of others, Lord Leggatt and the rest of the judges in the Supreme Court dismissed the appeal and held that uber drivers were in law "workers".

Comments

With the gig economy taking over a significant portion of the employment community, the courts were compelled to compose innovative and more complicated rules around worker status. Though we could also see past tests being applied, such as the control tests, which remains relevant. The original case report is significantly more dense than the current article before you, which was largely deducted to accommodate the style of the book. Those who are interested are suggested to read the original case report for more details around worker status and the gig-economy.

达到一定限度，将严重影响工作。

5. 优步会审查可使用的汽车类型并规定所有行程的路线。

6. 当应用程序中的评分系统达到一定数值时，将导致司机受到警告和终止其使用该应用程序的能力。

7. 优步将乘客和司机之间的通信限制在最低限度。

基于上述原因和大量其他原因，莱加特大法官和最高法院的其他法官驳回了上诉，并判定优步司机是法律上的“工人”。

案件评述

随着零工经济占据了就业领域的很大一部分，法院被迫围绕工人地位制定创新的、更复杂的规则。但是我们也可以看到过去的验证标准被应用，如控制验证标准，这仍然具有相关性。本案报告的原件中的信息比本文要密集得多，本文在很大程度上为了适应本书的风格而做出了删减。建议感兴趣的人阅读案例报告原件，从而了解有关工人身份和零工经济的更多细节。

Part Five: Selected Cases under Trust Law and Equity

第五部分：信托法和衡平法案例

案例 1　布里斯托和西区房屋协会诉莫休案

[1998] Ch 1 (1996)

案例 2　雷加尔（黑斯廷斯）有限公司诉格列佛案

[1967] 2 A.C.134

案例 3　鲍威尔诉康普顿等人案

[1945] Ch 123 (1944)

Case 1 Bristol & West Building Society v Mothew —The basics of trust and fiduciary duty

Preface:

Common Law has been under active development for numerous decades with its powers and justice being far reaching throughout the continents. In the UK, especially, the legal jurisdictions have relied heavily on common law to produce the most satisfactory of just results. However, UK law makers realized long ago that there are cases and situations which common law will not suffice, and from these realizations came the notion of Equity.

Specifically in this article I will discuss, with the assistance of a landmark case law an extremely central part of equity: Fiduciary duties and trust.

It may be beneficial to first uncover and basics of a fiduciary duty and how a fiduciary must act to be in accordance with his duties.

案例1 布里斯托和西区房屋协会诉莫休案——信托与信义义务的基础

引言:

数十年来，普通法一直获得积极的发展，其力量和司法在各大洲影响深远。特别是在英国，司法管辖严重依赖普通法以产生最令人满意的公正结果。然而，英国立法者很早即意识到，有些案件和情形是普通法所不能满足的，并且从该认识中产生了衡平法的概念。

具体到本文中，笔者将在一个具有里程碑意义的案例法的帮助下讨论衡平法的一个极其核心的部分：信义义务和信托。

我们需要首先揭示信义义务的基础知识以及一名受托人必须如何按照其义务行事。

Fiduciary:

A fiduciary is an individual who has undertaken the duty to act for another (the principal) in some matters which give rise to a unique relationship of trust and confidence. In turn, he possesses certain duties which he is bound by: To act in good faith; no profit to be made by himself; must place himself in a situation where his interest and duty will not collide; he must act solely for the benefit of his principal and not for himself or any third party without express, and informed consent of his principal.

Facts

The defendant, Mr Mothew was a solicitor who had undertaken to act for Mr and Mrs Towers in the purchase of a house, for the sum of 73, 000 pounds. He also acted on behalf of the plaintiff, Bristol and West Building Society ("the Society"), which acted as the lender and would forward to Mr and Mrs Towers an advance of 59, 000 pounds in mortgage to finance the purchase of the property. In the application by the Towers, they stated that the last 14, 000 pounds would be coming from their own pockets and would not be coming from another source of financial assistance.

The mortgage was subsequently advanced by the Society to the Towers under the express condition that the balance of the purchase price must come from the Towers' personal account and not another borrowing method. The Society gave the following instructions

受托人：

受托人是为另一人（委托人）承担执行某些事项的义务并形成一种独特的信任和保密关系。相应地，他具有特定的义务且受约束于：诚信地行事；不得自行获利；必须使自己处于利益和责任不相冲突的境地；未经委托人明确和知情同意，他必须仅为其委托人的利益行事，不得为自己或任何第三方行事。

案件事实

被告莫休先生是一名事务律师，曾承诺代表托尔斯夫妇购买一栋价值 7.3 万英镑的房屋。他也同时为原告布里斯托和西区房屋协会（以下简称该协会）行事，该协会作为贷款人，将向托尔斯夫妇发放 59，000 英镑的抵押贷款，以资助后者购买该财产。在托尔斯夫妇提交的申请中，他们说明，最后 1.4 万英镑将由其自有资金支付，不会来自其他财务援助来源。

随后，该协会向托尔斯夫妇支付抵押贷款，明确的条件是购买价格的余额必须来自托尔斯夫妇的个人账户，而非其他借款方式。该协会向被告莫休先生发出以下指示，说明他作为律师必须提交的内容：

to the defendant Mr Mothew on what he, as their solicitor must provide:

"Any proposal that the applicant may create a second mortgage or enter into a promissory note or otherwise borrow in order to finance part of the purchase price. (ix) Any incorrect information given in the solicitor's instructions. (x) Any other matters which ought to be brought to the notice of the Society..." Mr Mothew as a solicitor must submit an honest report that to the best of his knowledge, his other principal, the Towers would not request further borrowing for the purchase of the property.

Mr and Mrs Towers decided to provide the balance of the price by means of the net proceeds of sale of their last property. Though it was discovered that they had a subsisting mortgage owed to Barclays Bank on that property which after being paid, left them having to secure a second charge on the new property due to an insufficient amount of funds. They agreed with the bank that 3350 pounds out of the whole debt could remain unpaid after the sale of their last property and this amount will be secured by the second charge on the new property. The defendant was informed of this decision, it was apart of his duty as a solicitor to inform the Society about this further borrowing. Unfortunately, he either forgot due to an oversight or for other reasons, he did not report the 3350 pounds charge to the Society. A while later the Society was informed of the second charge by the defendant and it approved the charge rather easily.

Ultimately the purchasers Mr and Mrs Towers defaulted on their repayments and the Society had to enforce its rights to sell

“任何提议，即申请人可能设定第二笔抵押贷款或签署本票或以其他方式借款，以支付部分买价。(ix) 律师指示中的任何错误信息。(x) 应引起该协会注意到的任何其他事项……”作为律师，莫休先生必须提交一份尽其所知的诚实的报告，声明他的另一位委托人，托尔斯夫妇不会为了购买该财产而要求进一步借款。

托尔斯夫妇决定以出售他们此前房产获得的净收益来支付余款。但是发现他们对巴克莱银行的抵押贷款仍然存在，在支付抵押贷款后，由于资金不足，他们不得不在新房产上设定第二个权益。他们与银行达成协议，在出售上一处房产后，全部债务中剩下的 3350 英镑可以不用付清，这笔款项将由在新房产上设置的第二个权益予以担保。被告获知这项决定，作为律师的职责之一，他应通知该协会有关该进一步借款的事宜。不幸的是，由于疏忽或其他原因，他没有向该协会报告 3350 英镑的权益设置。其后不久，被告向该协会通知了第二个权益设定的事项，该协会很轻易就批准了这个设定的权益。

最终，购房者托尔斯夫妇拖欠还款，该协会不得不强制执行其出售房产的权利。该协会以 53,000 英镑的价格出售了该

the property. The Society sold the property for 53, 000 pounds, meaning they suffered at least 6000 pounds loss. The Society had since claimed to recover their loss from the defendant Mr Mothew, on the basis of breach of contract, negligence and breach of trust.

Issue

1. What are fiduciary duties and its breaches?

2. Can a fiduciary act for two principals simultaneously in the same transaction?

3. When is a trust breached?

Judicial View

Arguments on whether the Society would still have proceeded with the mortgage:

The defendant argued that even if he did include in his report that the Towers were under a further charge to the bank, the Society would not be concerned by this. He stated that in 1988 the property market was on the rise and the mortgage lenders were beyond willing to advance money to house purchasers. This was shown by the lack of concern displayed by the Society when they learned the existence of the second charge.

The case was first heard by the district court who decided that the defendant was liable to the breach of contract, negligence

处房产，这意味着他们至少损失了 6000 英镑。该协会其后以违反合约、疏忽及违反信托为由，向被告莫休先生追讨他们的损失。

争议焦点

1. 什么是信义义务及其违反行为？
2. 受托人能否在同一交易中同时代表两个委托人行事？
3. 信托在什么情况下会被违反？

司法观点

关于该协会是否仍会办理抵押贷款的论点：

被告辩称，即使他在报告中指出托尔斯夫妇有一项针对银行的权益设置，该协会也不会对此感到担忧。他指出，1988 年房地产市场正在上升，抵押贷款机构极其愿意向购房者出借款项。当他们得知第二个权益设置存在时，该协会看似毫不在乎的表现就表明了这一点。

地区法院首先审理此案并判定被告应承担违约、疏忽和违反信托的责任。为了明确起见，本文不会分开一审法院和上诉

and breach of trust. For the purpose of clarity, this article will not discuss the judgment of the first instance court and the court of appeal distinctly but instead together.

Millett LJ in the court of appeal approached the case with two focus points: the claims available in common law and the claims in equity. I will omit his reasoning for common law to stay true to the focus of this article (Equity), though you can find the summary of the judgment as follows:

The Society successfully established a causal link between Mr Mothew's negligence and the loss, though they have yet to discover the real amount of its loss which was caused by the defendant's negligence. The damages may be assessed in the future for breach of contract and negligence.

The claims in equity:

To aid your understanding of fiduciary relationship in equity, the relationship between the three parties is as follows:

The defendant Mr Mothew acted as the fiduciary for both the Society and the Towers, making both parties his principal. The 59,000 pounds transferred from the Society to the Towers was the "Trust Property".

The first instance judge found that the defendant was liable to a breach of trust by applying for the mortgage on behalf of the Towers and he must restore the entirety of the trust property with interest due to these reasons:

"[the defendant] received the cheque... for £59,000 as a

法院的判决，而是将二者结合起来讨论。

上诉法院的米利特大法官以两个焦点处理该案：普通法下的主张和衡平法下的主张。为了本文对衡平法的聚焦，笔者将省略他关于普通法的解释，但是您可以在以下找到判决的摘要：

该协会成功地确定了莫休先生的过失与其损失之间的因果关系，但是他们尚未确定由被告过失造成的损失的实际数额。该损失未来将因违约和疏忽而进行评估。

衡平法下的主张：

为了帮助您理解衡平法中的受托关系，本案三方之间的关系说明如下：

被告莫休先生是该协会和托尔斯夫妇的受托人，双方均是他的委托人。从该协会转移到托尔斯夫妇的59,000英镑是"信托财产"。

一审法官裁定，被告代表托尔斯夫妇申请抵押贷款，因违反信托义务而负有责任，因此必须归还全部信托财产并支付利息，原因如下：

［被告］收到59,000英镑支票的直接原因是他向该协

direct result of the misleading report which he had supplied to the Society... The money was paid... as a result of a misrepresentation made to the Society by the defendant... from the moment when [the] cheque for £59,000 was received by [the defendant] he held it upon a constructive trust to return it forthwith to the Society."

Since the district court judge believed that the sole reason Mr Mothew received the trust property was due to his misrepresentationand when he transferred the money to the vendors of the house instead of returning it, it constituted a breach of trust. The judge thought that it was crucial whether the defendant knew of the second charge, which he did. The judge stated that the defendant *"knew or must be taken to have known"* the existence of the second charge and had since provided misleading information to the Society, in turn breaching his fiduciary duty.

Millett LJ in the court of appeal was not convinced by this. He began his analysis on the sentence *"knew or must be taken to have known"*. Millett LJ believed that this was not an accurate description of the facts of the case. He argued that the more suitable phrase was *"knew or ought to have known"*. The difference between the two was that the information of the second charge was not present in the defendant's mind when writing the report. Therefore, he could not have been considered to *"know or taken to have known"*, but only that he *"ought to have known"*.

Millett LJ maintained that it was never alleged that the defendant concealed the second charge on purpose to intentionally mislead the Society, which in consequence making his breach of duty unconscious. He stated, *"I would not willingly treat such*

会提供了误导性的报告……由于被告向该协会作了虚假陈述……支付了款项……从［被告］收到59,000英镑支票的那一刻起他就以推定信托的方式持有并需立即将其归还该协会。

由于地区法院法官认为，莫休先生收到信托财产的唯一原因是他的失实陈述，当他将钱转移给房屋的卖主而不是返还时，即构成了违反信托。法官认为，至关重要的是被告是否知道第二个设定的权益，而他确实知道。法官论及，被告“知道或必须被视为已经知道”第二个设定的权益的存在，并且此后向该协会提供了误导性信息，从而违反了他的信义义务。

上诉法院的米利特大法官对此并不信服。他首先分析了“知道或必须被视为已经知道”这句话。米利特大法官认为，这不是对案件事实的准确描述。他认为更合适的措辞是“知道或应该知道”。二者的区别在于，被告在撰写报告时，并未想到第二个设定的权益的信息。因此，他不能被认为是“知道或被视为知道”，而只能被认定为他“应该知道”。

米利特大法官坚持认为，被告从未受到隐瞒第二个设定的权益且目的是故意误导该协会的指控，这意味着其是在没有意识到的情况下违反了义务。他认为：“除非有权威先例强迫这样做，我不愿意将该种行为视为违反信托或滥用信托资金，而且

conduct as involving a breach of trust or misapplication of trust money unless compelled by authority to do so, and in my judgment neither principle nor authority compels such a conclusion."

On fiduciary duty:

Millett LJ moved on to the discussion on whether the defendant was in breach of any fiduciary duties. Millett LJ delivered an informative judgment on this segment which aided the overall definition and understanding of fiduciary duties. He argued, *"The expression 'fiduciary duty' is properly confined to those duties which are peculiar to fiduciaries and the breach of which attracts legal consequences differing from those consequent upon the breach of other duties."* This clarification by Millett LJ formed the helpful phrase which every law student was expected to remember: *"Not every breach of duty by a fiduciary is a breach of fiduciary duty."*

Millett LJ cited a part of the judgment by Lord Browne-Wilkinson in *Henderson v. Merrett Syndicates Ltd. [1995] 2 A.C. 145*, which stated, *"[Fiduciary duty] arises from the circumstances in which the defendants were acting, not from their status or description."* This can be taken to mean that fiduciary duties only arise as a result of specific circumstances, but not just because one is a fiduciary.

With the definition clarified, Millett LJ began to list a couple of fiduciary duties which was worth discussing depending on the context of the present case.

在我看来，原则和权威先例均不强迫这样做。”

关于信义义务：

米利特大法官接着讨论被告是否违反了任何信义义务。米利特大法官就这一部分作出了信息丰富的判决，且有助于全面定义和理解信义义务。他认为，“‘信义义务’一词适当地限于受托人特有的义务，违反这些义务所引起的法律后果与违反其他义务所产生的法律后果不同”。米利特大法官的这一澄清形成了一个有用的短语，每个法律专业的学生均应该记住：“并非受托人违反任何一个义务的行为均是违反了信义义务。”

米利特大法官引用了布朗恩·威尔金森大法官在亨德森诉梅里特联合有限公司案（[1995] 2 A.C.145）中的部分判决，其中指出，“[信义义务] 产生于被告行事时的情况，而不是来源于其身份或描述”。这可以被理解为，信义义务只是在特定情况下产生，而不仅仅是因为一个人是受托人。

随着定义的澄清，米利特大法官开始列出一些值得根据本案背景讨论的信义义务。

The double employment rule:

The first instance court argued that the cause of any breach of fiduciary duty claims for this case was that the defendant acted as a fiduciary for both the Society and the Towers. This was due to the "obligation of undivided loyalty", which would be in breach of when a fiduciary acts, without the informed consent of both, for two principals simultaneously, who may potentially possess conflicting interests. Millett LJ did not believe this was relevant since it was perfectly clear upon the facts that the Society knew that Mr Mothew was acting for the Towers. The Society argued, while this is true, the Society was not informed of the arrangements on the second charge, so they were not "fully informed". Millett LJ countered this argument by stating that the Society was indeed fully informed of all relevant facts which could have affected their choice of solicitor. He submitted, *"its earlier decision to employ the defendant despite the potentially conflicting interest of his other clients was a fully informed decision."*

The good faith rule:

Millett LJ continued as he stated that another layer of fiduciary duty for the defendant is that he must act in good faith when acting as a fiduciary for both principals, he must take care of the interests of each and must not act in a way which furthers the interest of one to the prejudice of another. When applying this to the case,

双重雇佣准则：

一审法院认为，本案中任何违反信义义务主张的原因是被告同时作为该协会和托尔斯夫妇的受托人。这是源于“绝对忠诚的义务”，如果一个受托人未经双方知情同意，同时为两个可能拥有冲突利益的委托人行事，将违反绝对忠诚义务。米利特大法官并不认为这具有相关性，因为事实上很清楚，该协会知晓莫休先生是为托尔斯夫妇工作。该协会认为，虽然这是事实，但该协会没有被告知关于第二个权益的安排，因此他们没有“完全知情”。米利特大法官反驳了这一论点，指出该协会确实充分了解了可能影响其选择律师的所有相关事实。他认为：“**尽管其与被告的其他客户可能存在利益冲突，但该协会早些时候还是决定雇用被告，这是一个充分知情的决定。**”

诚信准则：

米利特大法官接着论及，被告的另一层信义义务是，他必须诚信行事，作为两个委托人的受托人行事时，他必须顾及每个委托人的利益，不得以促进一方利益而损害另一方利益的方式行事。在将这一点适用于本案时，米利特大法官称，当被告在报告中遗漏了关于第二个设定的权益的信息时，他是在

Millett LJargued that when the defendant left out the information on the second charge in the report, he did so unconsciously and an unconscious omission which consequently *"benefits one principal at the expense of another"* does not in equity constitute any breach of fiduciary duty.

The actual conflict rule:

The final duty discussed by Millett LJ was the actual conflict rule, the duty to avoid any actual conflict between the principals which may negatively influence his ability to fulfil his obligations to oneprinciple without failing in another. In situations like these the fiduciary must cease acting for one, or both principals to avoid further conflicts of interest.

The first instance judge thought that the defendant abused his fiduciary relationship with the Towers to obtain some level of benefit at the expense of the Society, and stated, *"First, in Mothew, the 'agent' was a fiduciary who had put himself in a position in which his duty to the lender was in conflict with the interests of his other client, the borrower"*. Millett LJ disagreed with this idea and instead argued that the defendant's duties to the Towers doesn't negative his duties to provide truthful information to the Society, that he did not act in bad faith and the purchasers did not require him to abuse their fiduciary relationship, nor did he intend to do so. Ultimately Millett LJ held that the defendant was not in breach of any fiduciary duties owed to the plaintiff.

无意识中这样做的，因此“**使一名委托人受益而牺牲另一名委托人**”的无意识遗漏在衡平法上并不构成任何违反信义义务的行为。

实际冲突准则：

米利特大法官讨论的最后一项义务是实际冲突准则，即避免委托人之间任何实际冲突的义务，这种冲突可能使他对一名委托人履行义务而不违反另一名委托人义务的能力产生负面影响。在该种情况下，受托人必须停止为一位或两位委托人行事，以避免进一步的利益冲突。

一审法官认为，被告滥用其与托尔斯夫妇的受托关系，以牺牲该协会为代价获取某种程度的利益，并指出，“**首先，在莫休案中，‘代理人’是一名受托人，他将自己置于这样一种境地，即他对贷款人的义务与其另一个客户即借款人的利益相冲突**”。米利特大法官不同意这一观点，相反，他认为被告对托尔斯夫妇的义务并不否定他向该协会提供真实信息的义务，他没有恶意行事，买方也没有要求他滥用他们的受托关系，他也没有打算这样做。最终，米利特大法官认为被告没有违反对原告负有的任何信义义务。

Breach of trust:

The first instance judge believed there to be a breach of trust. This is due to the opinion that the defendant acted as a trustee for the trust property (59,000 pounds) for the Society, and that his authority to deal with the money was in fact vitiated since the trust property was obtained by him by misrepresentation. Millett LJ believed otherwise, he started by stating that Mr Mothew never possessed any interests in the trust property which may benefit him in any way and the property remained in equity to the Society the entire time. Moreover, Millett LJ explained, *"Misrepresentation makes a transaction voidable not void. It gives the representee the right to elect whether to rescind or affirm the transaction,"* and since there were no action by the Society to do so, the trust was not void.

Ultimately, Millett LJ, and the rest of the judges who agreed with him, allowed the appeal and held that the defendant Mr Mothew was not in breach of any fiduciary duty. The claims in common law on negligence and breach of contract awaits further consideration on the amount of damages owed.

Comments

Fiduciary duty and trust are tricky doctrines in the notion of equity, with the cases usually involving complicated relationships between parties. Millett LJ and the court of appeal in the present

信托的违反：

一审法官认为存在违反信托的行为。这是因为认为被告为该协会担任信托财产（59,000英镑）的受托人，但是由于信托财产是由他通过虚假陈述获得的，因此他处理这笔钱的权力实际上是无效的。米利特大法官则持相反观点，他首先指出，莫休先生从未拥有信托财产中可能以任何方式使他受益的任何权益，并且该财产始终在衡平法下属于该协会。此外，米利特大法官解释说，“虚假陈述使交易可无效，而不是无效。它赋予被代理人选择是否撤销或确认交易的权利”，由于该协会没有采取行动，信托并未无效。

最终，米利特大法官和其他同意他的法官支持了上诉，并认为被告莫休先生没有违反任何信义义务。普通法中关于疏忽和违约的主张有待于对损害赔偿数额的进一步衡量。

案件评述

在衡平法概念中，信义义务和信托是一种棘手的学说，其案例通常涉及当事人之间的复杂关系。米利特大法官和上诉法院在本案中做出了巨大努力，以澄清并非受托人所负有的每项

case put in great effort to clarify that not every duty owed by a fiduciary comes under fiduciary duties and analysed three major fiduciary duties as explained above. Cases such as the one before us are crucial to the development of equity and to the betterment of the overall understanding of its legal powers.

义务均属于信义义务，并分析了上述三项主要的信义义务。我们面前的这类案件对于发展衡平法和增进对其法律权力的全面了解至关重要。

Case 2 Regal (Hastings) Ltd v Gulliver

—Can fiduciaries make profits from his/her position?

Preface:

The rules on equity and fiduciary relationship are much wider than what was discussed in the last article. In the present one I hope, with the assistance from a landmark case decided by the House of Lords, to discuss one of the more controversial duties of a fiduciary: the no-profit rule. It surely is understandable that any man would be a fool to turn back on opportunities to make profits, especially if it was made in good conscience with no intention of deceit. However, this may not always be the case when one is placed in the position of a fiduciary, in turn creating the problematic question which attracts a devoid of controversial answers: can a fiduciary make profits from his position?

Facts

Please note that the facts of the following case are of a unique

案例 2　雷加尔（黑斯廷斯）有限公司诉格列佛案
——受托人能否从其职位中获利？

引言：

衡平法与信义关系下的准则比上一篇文章所讨论的要宽泛得多。在本篇中，笔者希望在上议院裁决的一个具有里程碑意义的案件的协助下，讨论一个更具争议性的受托人义务：无利润准则。当然可以理解的是，任何一个拒绝机会赚取利润的人就是一个傻瓜，特别是，如果他是出于良心且没有欺骗的意图。然而，当一个人处于受托人的地位时，情况可能并不总是如此，这相应地又产生了一个棘手的问题，而这个问题存在诸多具有争议性的答案：受托人能否从他的职位中获利？

案件事实

请注意，以下案例的事实具有独特的性质，法律学者通常

nature and its details are usually regarded by legal learners as ambiguous.

The appellant is Regal Ltd ("Regal"), which owned and managed one cinema and whose board of five directors were Walter Bentley, Gulliver, Bobby, Griffiths and Bassett.

During 1935 the board formed a scheme for acquiring two more cinemas by lease owned by another company. Though the lease was not to be granted directly to Regal, but a subsidiary limited Company to be formed by Regal, named Amalgamated Ltd. The subsidiary required a capital of 5000 pounds shares to be purchased by Regal, making it the only owner of all 5000 shares. A few months passed and Walter Bently had passed away, with his Son Harry Bently now appointed as director alongside the four previously existing directors, forming a new board. In that same month Regal was considering, together with the acquisition of the leasehold cinemas, a sale of its own cinema, and the leasehold interest of the two cinemas when acquired. Regal's solicitor Garton was instructed that the directors of Regal were willing to provide a joint guarantee of the rent of the two cinemas, up until the previously agreed capital of 5000 pounds were paid up by Regal to Amalgamated. In the same year, Amalgamated Ltd, the proposed subsidiary was registered, with its directors being the five existing directors of Regal and the solicitor Garton.

However, Regal soon realized that they were unable to pay for the whole of the 5000 shares, so they formed a new financial plan

认为其细节模棱两可。

上诉人为雷加尔有限公司（以下简称雷加尔公司），其拥有并管理一家电影院，董事会由沃尔特·本特利、格列佛、鲍比、格里菲斯和巴塞特组成。

1935年，董事会制订了一项计划，以租赁方式收购另一家公司所有的两家电影院。但是租赁并不直接授予雷加尔公司，而将属于雷加尔公司即将设立的一家名为“联合有限公司”的子公司。该子公司的成立需要雷加尔公司购买5000英镑的股份，使其成为所有5000股股份的唯一所有者。几个月过后，沃尔特·本特利去世了，他的儿子哈里·本特利现在被任命为董事，与之前的4位董事一起组成新一届董事会。同月，雷加尔公司在考虑在收购租赁电影院的同时，拟出售自己的电影院以及待收购的两家电影院的租赁权益。雷加尔公司的律师加顿被指示，在雷加尔公司向联合有限公司支付之前约定的5000英镑股份前，雷加尔公司的董事愿意为两家电影院的租金提供联合担保。同年，拟议子公司联合有限公司被注册成立，其董事为雷加尔公司的5名现任董事及其律师加顿。

然而，雷加尔公司很快意识到，其无力支付全部5000股本，因此，他们为联合有限公司的形成制订了一个新的财务计

for the establishment of Amalgamated, of the 5000, 2000 were to be subscribed by Regal and the remainder be allocated to Regal or its nominees. This meant that Regal would only own 2000 shares of Amalgamated instead of the whole, as planned previously.

The most vital change of events happened in the afternoon of October 2, 1935, where Garton and the five directors met at their registered office and held a meeting where they discussed extensively regarding the impending sale. Decisions were made and it would seem from the records that two separate meetings were held that day, one was by the board of Regal and the other by the board of Amalgamated, the only difference in participants was the addition of Garton the solicitor in the second meeting since he was one of the directors of Amalgamated.

From the mixed evidence and records, it was upon the facts that these are the main decisions made during the two meetings: (1) Regal could only afford to provide 2000 pounds out of 5000 for the shares capital in Amalgamated; (2) Since Regal could not afford the whole of the 5000 pound shares, the rest were to be paid and allotted to the 6 directors of Amalgamated, with 500 each.

By October 7 the lease of the two cinemas was executed and the shares were allotted as follows: 2000 to Regal as previous agreed upon, 500 to each of the five directors Bobby, Griffiths, Bassett, Bentley and Garton. As for the sixth director Gulliver, who rejected to pay the 500, his part was paid up by two other companies (200 each) and an individual (100) under his direction.

However, contrary to what was previously discussed and

划，5000 股中的 2000 股将由雷加尔公司购入，其余分配给雷加尔公司或其提名人。这意味着，雷加尔公司将只拥有 2000 股联合有限公司的股份，而不是之前计划的全部股份。

最重要的变化发生在 1935 年 10 月 2 日下午，加顿和 5 位董事在他们的注册办公室会面并召开了一次会议，就即将进行的出售进行了深入讨论。他们随即做出了一些决定，从记录中可以看出，当天举行了两次单独的会议，一次由雷加尔公司董事会召开，另一次由联合公司董事会召开。两次会议参与者的唯一区别是第二次会议增加了加顿律师，因为他是联合有限公司董事之一。

从混杂的证据、记录和事实看，两次会议期间做出的主要决定为：（1）雷加尔公司只能支付 5000 英镑中的 2000 英镑作为联合有限公司的股份；（2）由于雷加尔公司无法支付全部 5000 英镑的股份，其余的将被分配给联合有限公司的 6 名董事支付，每人 500 英镑。

截至 10 月 7 日，两家电影院的租约已签订，股份分配如下：2000 股按先前约定分配给雷加尔公司，500 股分配给鲍比、格里菲斯、巴塞特、本特利和加顿 5 位董事。至于拒绝支付 500 英镑的第六位董事格列佛，他的部分由另外两家公司（每家 200 英镑）和一名个人（100 英镑）基于其指示而支付。

然而，与之前讨论并接受的关于出售 3 家电影院的计划相

accepted plan on selling the three cinemas, a proposition was accepted by the Amalgamated Directors that there would be a purchase, from the individuals (directors of Amalgamated) their shares in Regal and Amalgamated. The 2700 shares held by the 5 directors of Amalgamated and the 300 held by Gulliver's nominees were bought with nearly 3 pound per share purchase price and parts of the profits of the sale were attributed to the directors personally.

As a result of the sale of shares, Regal had to replace the former directors with a new board, who, representing Regal initiated this litigation. Regal claimed to recover from the five former directors and Garton, the former solicitor the profits made from their previous sale, making the five directors and Garton, joint together as 6 defendants.

Issue

1. Are directors trustees of their company?

2. If so, had the directors breached their fiduciary duties to the company?

Judicial View

Decisions of the three courts (High court/Court of Appeal/ House of Lords):

For the purpose of continuity, I shall discuss the judgment of

反，联合有限公司的董事会接受了一项提议，即将从个人（联合有限公司董事）购买他们在雷加尔公司和联合有限公司的股份。联合有限公司的 5 名董事持有的 2700 股股份以及格列佛的提名人拥有的 300 股股份以每股近 3 英镑的收购价购入，部分出售利润归董事个人所有。

由于股份的出售，雷加尔公司必须以新董事会取代前董事会，新董事会代表雷加尔公司提起诉讼。雷加尔公司主张向 5 位前董事和加顿（前律师）追讨其先前出售的利润，5 位董事和加顿成为 6 名共同被告。

争议焦点

1. 董事是公司的受托人吗？
2. 如是，董事是否违反了其对公司的信义义务？

司法观点

三个法院（高等法院 / 上诉法院 / 上议院）的判决：

为了文章的连续性，我将以与上一篇文章类似的方式一并

the three courts congruently, in a similar manner as the last article. Though I will first address the decisions of both the trial judge and the judges in the court of appeal which all held for the respondents in this case.

The first instance judge approached the matter with a specified focus on the intention of the 6 defendants. The judge stated, *"if the plaintiffs can establish that, though no loss was made by the company, yet a profit was corruptly made by the directors and the solicitor, then the company can claim to have that profit handed over to the company."* From the diction of "corruptly", one can infer that the judge meant to suggest that if Regal was able to prove, upon facts or otherwise that the respondents had acted mala fide in the process of obtaining these profits, they would succeed in such a claim. It was subsequently found that the respondents acted bona fide, for the interest of Regal, and that there were no damages to be paid to Regal. The plaintiff had since appealed.

When the case reached the Court of Appeal, the judges took a completely different approach, when they put their focus on the duties of the directors. You may remember from the facts that Regal could not afford the whole of the 5000 shares capital for Amalgamated Ltd, with 3000 out of the 5000 being purchased by the directors. The Court of Appeal took the view that in order to succeed, Regal had to establish that the directors owed a duty to obtain the shares for Regal, meaning that if the duty was found to exist, the directors should have found other means, either by loans or sale of other properties to allow Regal to obtain the remaining 3000 shares, instead of purchasing it

讨论三个法院的判决。但是我将首先说明初审法官和上诉法院的法官判决结果：均判定本案被告胜诉。

一审法官在处理这一问题时特别关注了6名被告的意图。法官认为，“如果原告能够证明，虽然公司没有亏损，但各董事和律师却腐败地获利，那么公司可以主张将利润移交给公司”。从“腐败地”一词可以推断，法官的意思是如果雷加尔公司能够根据事实或其他渠道证明，被告在获取这些利润的过程中存有恶意行为，他们的主张将会成功。其后发现，被告的行为善意，是为了雷加尔公司的利益，无须向雷加尔公司支付任何损害赔偿金。原告之后提出了上诉。

当案件被移送至上诉法院时，法官们采取了完全不同的做法，他们将重点放在董事的职责上。雷加尔公司无法承担联合有限公司的全部5000股，其中3000股由董事会购买。上诉法院认为，如果雷加尔公司想成功主张，他们必须确定董事有义务为雷加尔公司获得股份，这意味着如果发现该义务存在，董事应通过贷款或出售其他财产找到其他手段帮助雷加尔公司获得剩余的3000股股份，而不是自己购买。上诉法院的格林大法官认为，“据说，在本案的情况下，董事在获得这些股份时，必须被视为在履行其职务；因此，他们应对自己所获得的利润负责”。最后，格林大法官认为，自从各董事（和律师加顿）

themselves. Lord Greene of the Court of Appeal argued, *"It is said that, in the circumstances of the case, the directors must be taken to have been acting in the matter of their office when they took those shares; and that accordingly they are accountable for the profits which they have made."* Ultimately, Lord Greene argued that since the moment the directors (and Garton the solicitor) took from their own pockets and bought the remaining shares, the duty ceased to exist. The Court of Appeal dismissed Regal's appeal and the matter was again appealed to the House of Lords.

You may wonder, at this point of reading, how is this case related to Equity and Trust? This is precisely what the first and second instance courts incorrectly omitted. The two courts focused solely on the potential wrongdoings of the directors in common law, but failed to recognize the possibility that the directors might have been acting as fiduciaries of Regal, meaning that they were potentially liable under the equitable breach of fiduciary duty.

Lord Russell in the House of Lords began his reasoning by rejecting the "mala fide or bona fide" argument considered by the High Court, as he submitted that the intentions of the directors *were "irrelevant to a claim against a person occupying a fiduciary relationship towards the plaintiff for an account of the profits made by that person by reason and in course of that relationship."* After rejecting the approached taken by the High Court, Lord Russell moved on to the "duty argument" by the Court of Appeal and addressed the key problem subsisting in both initial judgments, *"The rule of equity which insists on those, who by use of a fiduciary position*

自己出资购买剩余股份，这项义务就不复存在了。上诉法院驳回了雷加尔公司的上诉，其再次向上议院提出上诉。

阅读到此处时，您可能会想，这个案例与衡平法和信托有何关系？这正是一审和二审法院错误地忽略了的地方。两级法院仅关注普通法中董事潜在的不当行为，但未能认识到董事可能作为雷加尔公司的受托人行事的可能性，这意味着他们可能在衡平法下违反信义义务。

上议院的罗素大法官在开始分析时就拒绝了接受高等法院审议的“恶意或善意”论点，因为他认为，董事会的意图“与针对一个与原告拥有受托关系的人的主张无关，如果该人是在这种关系和过程中且合理获得利润的”。罗素大法官驳回了高等法院采取的做法后，又转到上诉法院的“责任论点”，并解决了两个最初判决中存在的关键问题，“衡平法准则坚持，那些利用受托地位获利的人有责任归还该利润，这不取决于欺诈或缺乏诚信……也不取决于受益人是否有义务为原告获得利润的来源……责任仅源于在所述情况下获利的事实，无论多么诚实和善意，均无法逃脱被要求承担责任的风险”。

make a profit, being liable to account for that profit, in no way depends on fraud, or absence of bona fides... or whether the profiteer was under a duty to obtain the source of the profit for the plaintiff... The liability arises from the mere fact of a profit having, in the stated circumstances, been made. The profiteer, however honest and well intentioned, cannot escape the risk of being called upon to account."

Lord Russell began his analysis on equity and fiduciary duty by the citation of a plethora of previous cases containing similar facts. To avoid unnecessary complexity and length of this article I will discuss only the one primary case which Lord Russell used.

Keech v Sandford:

In *Keech*, the defendant was acting as a trustee, holding the profits of a market for the benefit of an infant, though due to the infant's age, the renewal of the market's lease was unsuccessful. The trustee, realizing that it was impossible to fulfil his duties of a trustee by renewing for the benefit of the infant, took the lease for himself. The judge in this case decided that even if it was incapable for the infant to obtain the lease, the trustee was not allowed to obtain it for his own benefit, solely for the reason that he acted as the infant's trustee. The origin quote is as follows, *"This may seem hard, that the trustee is the only person of all mankind who might not have the lease: but it is very proper that the rule should be strictly pursued, and not in the least relaxed ..."* [4]

[4] Keech v Sandford, (1726) Sel Cas King 61.

罗素大法官在分析衡平法和信义义务时，首先引用了大量包含类似事实的先前案例。为了避免本文中出现不必要的复杂性和过长的篇幅，笔者将只讨论罗素大法官使用的一个主要案例。

基奇诉桑福德案：

在基奇案中，被告作为受托人，为一名婴儿的利益持有一个市场的利润权，但由于婴儿年幼，该市场的租约续期未获成功。受托人意识到其不可能履行其作为受托人为婴儿的利益续约的职责，因此为自己取得了租约。本案法官判定，即使该婴儿无能力获得租赁权，也不允许受托人为自己的利益获得租赁权，仅因其是该婴儿的受托人。原文引述如下："受托人是全人类唯一不能获得租赁权的人，这似乎很严厉；但严格执行这一规则是非常恰当的，丝毫不能放松……"[4]

[4] 基奇诉桑福德案，(1726) Sel Cas King 61。

With the no-profit rule examined, Lord Russell considered two essential elements which must be established in order to find the defendants liable for the profits which they made.

"By reason and in course of their office" :

The first element which Lord Russell identified was that the five respondents (excluding Garton since he was not a director of Regal) must have acquired the shares of Amalgamated Ltd *"by reason and in course of their office of directors of Regal."* For the first sub-element of "reason", Lord Russell believed that the 3000 pound shares no doubt had to be purchased by the directors themselves and Garton *"in their capacity as directors of Amalgamated"* due to the decision to purchase the leasehold interest of the two cinemas. For the second sub-element of "in their office of directors", Lord Russell stated that the decision to allow the directors to personally pay for the remaining 3000 shares was an action *"only the Regal directors could bring about"* and that this decision *"may not have been appreciated by them at the time; but its effect upon their company and its shareholders was striking."* Lord Russell meant to state that the scheme to purchase shares personally have directly led to the following consequences, Regal would not control the whole of Amalgamated Ltd or own the whole of its shares; The Regal shareholders would only receive a significantly reduced proportion of the money obtained from the sale of the two cinemas; and that the five former directors of Regal

罗素大法官在研究了无利润准则后，考虑了其必须确立的两个基本要素，以确定被告对其所获得的利润负有责任。

“合理和在其任职期间”：

罗素大法官确定的第一个要素是，5 名被告（不包括加顿，因为他不是雷加尔公司的董事）必须是“**合理且在其担任雷加尔公司董事职务时**”收购了联合有限公司的股份。对于“合理”这一首要元素，罗素大法官认为，由于决定购买两家电影院的租赁权，3000 英镑的股份无疑必须由董事和加顿“**以联合有限公司董事的身份**”购买。对于第二个元素“在其任职董事期间”，罗素大法官指出，允许董事个人支付剩余 3000 股款项的决定是“**只有雷加尔公司的董事才能采取的行动**”，而且这一决定“**当时可能没有得到他们的迎合；但其对公司及其股东的影响是惊人的**”。罗素大法官的意思是，个人购买股份的计划直接导致了以下后果：雷加尔公司不会完全控制联合有限公司或拥有其全部股份；雷加尔公司的股东只能从出售两家电影院的资金中获得大幅减少后的部分；雷加尔公司的 5 位前董事和律师加顿将收到雷加尔公司股东被剥夺的资金。最终，罗素大法官认为，第一个要素应该得到满足。

and Garton the solicitor would receive the money which were deprived of from the Regal shareholders. Ultimately it was in Lord Russell's opinion that this first element were to be satisfied.

The director's fiduciary identity:

The second element, and the more important one was that the directors must be in a fiduciary relationship with Regal in order for them to breach the no-profit rule. Lord Russell identified that this was a difficult question to answer, as he stated, *"Directors of a limited company are the creatures of statute and occupy a position peculiar to themselves. In some respects they resemble trustees, in others they do not. In some respects they resemble agents, in others they do not."* Lord Russell approached this issue with a similar fashion, where he cited judgments from previous cases concerning directors.

In *Parker v McKenna*, the directors of a company made profit by obtaining some shares that was not taken up by the shareholders. Lord Carins in Parker stated, *"All the court has to do is to examine whether a profit has been made by an agent, without the knowledge of his principal, in the course and execution of his agency."* [5] It is obvious that the directors were seen as agents in this case.

In Imperial Mercantile Credit Association (Liquidators) v. Coleman, the judge said, *"it is the duty of directors of companies to*

---

[5] [1874] 12 WLUK 35.

董事的受托身份：

第二个要素，也是更重要的一个要素是，如果主张董事违反无利润准则，他们必须与雷加尔公司存有受托关系。罗素大法官指出，这是一个很难回答的问题，正如他所说，“有限公司的董事是法定的，占据着自己特有的地位。在某些方面，他们类似于受托人，在另一些方面，他们不类似。在某些方面，他们类似于代理人，在另一些方面，并非如此”。罗素大法官以相似的方式处理这个问题，他引用此前有关董事的案件判决。

在帕克诉麦肯纳案中，一家公司的董事通过获得一些未被股东获得的股份而获利。卡林斯大法官在帕克案中指出，“法院所要做的就是审查代理人在其委托人不知情的情况下，在其代理过程和执行中是否获利”。[5]显然，在本案中，董事被视为代理人。

在帝国商业信用协会（清算人）诉科尔曼一案中，法官说：“公司董事有责任尽最大努力……且他们必须无视自己的私人

[5] [1874] 12 WLUK 35.

use their best exertions... and that they are bound to disregard their own private interests."[6]

As a result of the above cases and many others which I have omitted for ease of reading, Lord Russell in the present case found that the directors of Amalgamated was indeed involved in a fiduciary relationship to Regal. The respondents, Bobby, Griffiths, Bassett and Bentley are liable to account for the profit they made by selling their 500 shares in Amalgamated.

If you have read with care on the specific names of the respondents, you may realize that only four out of six were held liable from the above judgment. This is due to the fact that Lord Russell believed Gulliver, who rejected to pay the 500 shares and Garton, who only acted as a Solicitor of Regal, possessed unique qualities different from the other four, and their cases required further investigation.

Gulliver' s case:

Gulliver rejected to personally purchase 500 shares for Amalgamated and instead he requested two other companies, which he owned shares in and one of his personal friends to purchase the 500 shares. He stated, *"I never promised to subscribe for shares in Amalgamated. I never did so subscribe. I only promised to find others who would be willing to subscribe. I only found others who*

[6] Imperial Mercantile Credit Association (Liquidators) v. Coleman [1873] UKHL J0509-1.

利益。”[6]

由于上述案例以及为便于阅读而省略的许多其他案例，罗素大法官在本案中认定，联合有限公司的董事确实与雷加尔公司存在受托关系。被告鲍比、格里菲斯、巴塞特和本特利有责任归还出售联合有限公司每人 500 股股票所获得的利润。

如果您仔细阅读了被告的具体姓名，可能意识到，根据上述判决，6 名被告中只有 4 人负有责任。这是因为罗素大法官认为拒绝支付 500 股款项的格列佛和仅担任雷加尔公司律师的加顿具有不同于其他4人的特质，他们的案件需要进一步调查。

关于格列佛：

格列佛拒绝自己为联合有限公司购买 500 股股票，而是要求他拥有股份的另外两家公司和他的一位私人朋友购买这 500 股股票。他说：“我从来没有承诺过要认购联合有限公司的股份。我从来没有这样做过。我只承诺要找到其他愿意认购的人，我只是找到其他确实认购的人。这些股份是他们的。”原告认为，事实上这些股份仍然是他的，但罗素大法官认为，如果格列佛打算自己拥有这些股份，他没有理由隐瞒自己对这些

[6] 帝国商业信用协会（清算人）诉科尔曼案，[1873] UKHL J0509-1。

did subscribe. The shares were theirs." The plaintiffs believed that in reality the shares are still his, but Lord Russell argued that Gulliver had no reason to conceal his ownership of the shares if he intended to own them personally, since the directors had no reason to believe, when they purchased the shares that they would eventually be held liable to account for the profit made. Lord Russell examined the facts that found that Gulliver never owned any shares of Amalgamated personally and he never made any profits either.

Garton's case:

Garton the solicitor is unique to this case in a sense that he was only a director of Amalgamated, but not Regal. Upon the facts Lord Russell found that he was requested by Regal to apply for the 500 shares. Lord Russell approached Garton's case in a simple manner and stated, *"I know of no principle or authority which would justify a decision that a solicitor must account for profit resulting from a transaction which he has entered into on his own behalf, not merely with the consent, but at the request of his client."*

Ultimately, the House of Lords allowed part of the appeal for the appellant Regal and held that the four directors of Regal and Amalgamated save for Gulliver are to account for the profits made personally. The appeal was dismissed against the respondents Gulliver and Garton.

股份的所有权，因为董事们没有理由相信当他们购买这些股份时，他们最终会被要求对所获得的利润负责。罗素大法官调查事实后判定，格列佛从来没有个人拥有任何联合有限公司的股份，而且他从未获得任何利润。

关于加顿：

加顿律师在这个案件中很独特，因为他只是联合有限公司的董事，而非雷加尔公司的董事。根据事实罗素大法官发现，他是被雷加尔公司要求购入 500 股。罗素大法官以一种简单的方式处理了加顿的案件，并指出："据我所知，没有任何原则或权威先例能够证明律师必须归还其代表自己进行的交易所产生的利润这一决定是正当的，这种交易不仅是在征得同意的情况下进行的，而且是基于其委托人的要求。"

最终，上议院支持了上诉人雷加尔公司的部分上诉，并认为除去格列佛，雷加尔公司与联合有限公司的 4 名董事需归还其个人利润。针对被告格列佛和加顿的上诉被驳回。

Comments

The essence of this case came from the House of Lord's unanimous position towards one's inability to make profits when involved in a fiduciary relationship. We may infer from the House of Lord's judgment that the approach is a strict one, where in no circumstance can a fiduciary make personal profits without the express consent of their principal. Besides the no-profit rule, this judgment also reminds us of a significant character of common law: the courts are bound strictly by the judgments of precedents, meaning that the judges must exercise their discretion with extreme care and consideration, to avoid negative impacts upon future cases.

案件评述

本案的精华来自上议院对一个人在涉及受托关系时不能盈利的一致立场。我们可以从上议院的判决中推断，这种要求是严格的。没有委托人的明确同意，在任何情况下，受托人均不能获得个人利润。除了无利润准则外，这项判决还提醒我们普通法的一个重要特点：法院严格受判例判决的约束，这意味着法官必须极其谨慎且需慎重考虑如何行使其自由裁判权，以避免对今后的案件产生不利影响。

Case 3 Powell v Compton and Others
—What is "public" in charitable trusts?

Preface:

Trust is a complicated notion, I have not in the previous articles explained trusts in details, but instead focused on the explanation of fiduciary/trust relationship. With this article I hope to tackle a legal conundrum which had baffled legal learners of all generations: explaining trust, and more specifically, charitable trusts.

Here are some preliminary points to learn for the understanding of this article:

1. Charitable trusts are trusts established by a testatrix for the benefit of a section of public.

2. The rule against perpetuity limits all trusts to last a maximum of 80 years. Charitable trusts are the only exceptions.

Facts

The facts of each case in these articles, words which usually encourage readers and invite interest are, in this case I must

案例3　鲍威尔诉康普顿等人案
——慈善信托中的“公众”是什么？

引言：

信托是一个复杂的概念，在前面的文章中笔者并没有详细解释信托，而是侧重于解释信义/信托关系。在本文中，笔者希望去解决一个困扰了历代法律学习者的法律难题：解释信托，更具体来说，解释慈善信托。

以下是理解本文需要了解的一些初步要点：

1. 慈善信托是由立遗嘱人为一部分公众的利益而设立的信托。

2. 非永久性规则限制所有信托的存续期最长为80年。其中，唯一的例外就是慈善信托。

案件事实

笔者写的这些文章中的每一个案例事实，通常是鼓励读者和引起其兴趣的部分，但必须遗憾地承认，本文中的案件事实

regrettably confess, shockingly short and simple, which must be dealt with in a analytical manner:

A testatrix by will established a trust, intending it to possess a charitable nature, stated: *"... the money ... is to be ... invested ... under a trust for ever ... for the education of C. and P. and M. children but C. and P. children are to take the preference as scholarships for the time thought best by the trustees not over the age of twenty-six years. It is not to be used as a pension or income for anyone and is to be held as scholarships at the pleasure of the trustees. It is to be used to fit the children... serving the nation not as students for research of any kind."*

At first glance, one must focus on the following features of this trust:

1. The trust is meant to last indefinitely, and in order to do so must be recognized in equity as a valid charitable trust in order to pass the rule against perpetuities.

2. The beneficiaries are the descendants, irrespective of their wealth, of three families (C.P.M.).

3. The monetary benefits are to be arranged as "scholarships", possibly in the form of university tuition or private tutor.

4. The monetary benefits are not to be used in any other means save for educational purposes and this can be decided by the trustees.

5. The benefits are not to be used for research purposes but instead to ensure that the children may serve their nation well.

The testatrix passed away after establishing this charitable

非常短且简要，我们必须以分析的方式阅读：

立遗嘱人通过遗嘱设立信托，意图使其具有慈善性质，声明："……这笔钱……将……在一项信托下……永远……投资……用于C.和P.及M.的儿童的教育，但C.及P.儿童应在受托人认为最好的时间（不超过26岁）优先获得奖学金。这笔钱不得用作任何人的养老金或收入，并应作为奖学金由受托人之意持有。它是用来使孩子们……为国家服务，而不是为从事任何研究。"

首先，我们必须关注该信托的以下特征：

1. 该信托的目的为无限期持续，为了做到这一点，该信托必须在衡平法中被确认为有效的慈善信托，以通过非永久性规则。

2. 受益人是3个家庭的后裔，无论其财富如何（C.P.M.）。

3. 此金钱福利可能以大学学费或私人导师的形式，将被安排为"奖学金"。

4.除用于教育目的外，该金钱福利不得用于任何其他方式，这可由受托人决定。

5. 这些福利不是用于研究目的，而是为了确保儿童能够很好地为国家服务。

遗嘱人在设立该慈善信托后去世，遗嘱人在世的遗产代理

trust, and the surviving personal representatives of the testatrix hopes for the courts to clarify whether the trust was a valid one in terms of its charitable purposes or was it void. At the date of these events, there were in total twenty-eight children which fit the descriptions of a beneficiary in the will.

Issue

What are the mandatory requirements of a charitable trust?

Judicial View

The first instance decisions and the appeal:

The first instance judge, Cohen J held that the trust was indeed a valid one of charitable purpose as he was bound by the decisions of a multiplicity of established charitable trust cases which aimed to aid the poor relations of the testatrix. These cases are referred to as "the poor relations cases" which will be dealt with at the end of this article.

The next of kin for the testatrix appealed against this decision on the following grounds: In order for a charitable trust to be valid it must be for the benefit of a portion of public, and these three families concerned in the present case are not. This may be reasonable for poverty cases, since any pecuniary assistance towards poverty benefit the entire public, though the present case is

人希望法院澄清该信托在其慈善目的方面是有效的还是无效的。在这些事件发生之日，共有28名儿童符合遗嘱中受益人的描述。

争议焦点

慈善信托有哪些强制性规则？

司法观点

一审判决与上诉：

一审法官科恩法官认为，该信托确实是一个有效且为慈善目的设立的信托，因为他受到多个已确立的慈善信托案件裁决的约束，这些案件的目的是帮助与遗嘱人拥有关系且贫苦的人们。这些案件称为“贫困亲属案件”，将在本文末尾介绍。

遗嘱人的近亲对这一决定提出上诉，理由如下：为了使慈善信托有效，它必须为一部分公众的利益服务，而本案中涉及的这3个家庭则不然。这对于资助贫困案件来说可能是合理的，因为对贫困来说，任何金钱援助均有利于整个公众，但是目前的案件只涉及教育且仅惠及3个家庭。

concerned only with education, and this benefits the three families only.

The respondent's arguments are as follows: This case does involve the relief of poverty and if the appeal were to be allowed it would cast shadows on all cases on poverty relief. It is obvious from the diction of the bequest that the testator's aim was to educate the specified children of the three families so that they may, in the future be useful to the nation, this is a clear indication that the trust was established for the well-being of the entire nation, which sufficiently passes the "public" requirement of a charitable trust.

Court of Appeal decision:

Lord Greene in the Court of Appeal focused on three elements when assessing the present trust: Whether the trust in question passes the "public" test, what is the position that the courts usually take when assessing educational trusts, and finally the "poor relations cases" and how those cases influence the present trust. I will explain each of those three elements in turn.

Public:

The law requires all charitable trusts to benefit a substantial section of the public, the community or a section of the community. One may wonder, if so, does the number of beneficiaries matter? Lord Greene addressed this question by stating, *"it is not to be assumed that the number of potential beneficiaries will necessarily*

被申请人的论点如下：本案确实涉及对贫困的救济问题，如果支持上诉，则将对所有贫困救济案件造成阴影。从遗赠的措辞可以明显看出，遗嘱人的目的是教育这3个家庭的特定子女，以便他们将来对国家有用，这清楚地表明，信托是为整个国家的福祉而设立的，足以通过慈善信托的“公众”要求。

上诉法院判决：

上诉法院的格林大法官在评估该信托时关注了3个要素：所涉信托是否通过了“公众”验证标准，法院在评估教育信托时通常采取的立场是什么，最后关注了“贫困亲属案件”以及这些案件如何影响该信托。笔者将依次解释这3个要素中的每一个。

公众：

法律要求所有慈善信托均要惠及大部分公众、社区或社区的一部分。人们可能会想，如果是这样，受益人的数量是否重要？格林大法官在回答这个问题时说：“我们不能假定潜在受益人的数量总是很重要的。在任何情况下，仅仅是数量并不能将一个家庭或个人的捐赠提升到慈善捐赠的级别。”格林大法官

always be substantial. In any event, mere numbers cannot raise a family or private benefaction into the class of charitable gifts." What Lord Greene meant was that while numbers is relevant factor when considering charitable trusts, it cannot help a case when the trust is in its nature a private one, signifying that if one testator leaves property for the benefit of his 100 children, this may not be misled by the size of the beneficiary pool and be recognized as a charitable trust. Lord Greene believed that an addition of any private element is fatal to the constitution of a charitable trust, I will aid your understanding with a simple example: If a proposed charitable trust were aimed to benefit the poor residents of Town A, then the residents will receive benefits, not by their identities as an individual A, B, or C, but by their status as a resident in the larger community of town A. If, when asserting their claim to the trust, it appeared necessary for them to prove that they were individuals A, B, or C, it was of Lord Greene's opinion that, *"I cannot help thinking that on principle the gift ought not to be held to be a charitable gift, since the introduction into their qualification of a purely personal element would deprive the gift of its necessary public character."* Lord Greene further argued that if it was not necessary for them to establish themselves as A, B, or C, but instead ones related to A, B, or C, either their children or employees, this would also defeat the charitable trust as a purely personal element has been entered into. For the present case, the trust is directed towards the children of the three families and the current number is 28, some may argue that the fact that this number may change and fluctuate in the future,

的意思是，虽然在考虑慈善信托时数字是相关因素，但在信托性质为私人信托的情况下，数字无助于解决问题，这意味着如果一个遗嘱人为了 100 个子女的利益而留下财产，不能被受益人池的规模所误导而被确认为慈善信托。格林大法官认为，增加任何私人因素对慈善信托的成立均是致命的，笔者将用一个简单的例子帮助理解：如果拟议的慈善信托旨在惠及 A 镇的贫困居民，那么居民将获得利益，不是通过他们作为个人 A、B 或 C 的身份，但根据他们在 A 镇更大社区中的居民身份，如果他们在主张信托权利时，似乎有必要证明他们是 A、B 或 C 个人，格林大法官认为，“**我禁不住想，原则上不应将赠物视为慈善赠物，因为在他们的资格中引入纯粹个人因素将剥夺赠物必要的公共性质**”。格林大法官进一步指出，如果他们没有必要将自己确定为 A、B 或 C，而是与 A、B 或 C 相关的人，无论是他们的子女还是雇员，都会挫败慈善信托，因为已经融入了纯粹的个人要素。就目前的情况而言，信托针对的是 3 个家庭的子女且目前的数字是 28，有些人可能会认为，这一数字在未来可能发生变化和波动，可能成为一个更大的群体，从而可能被视为公众的一部分。但是格林大法官认为，“**在个人因素构成资格的重要部分的情况下，所涉及的人数可能很大，这一事实在我看来对所适用的原则没有任何影响……我认为，无论这种关系的近疏，无论是限于一代人还是扩展到两个或 3 个或永久，结果均会相同**”。

to become possibly a larger group of individuals may be seen as a portion of the public, though Lord Greene argued, *"The fact that in cases where a personal element forms an essential part of the qualification the numbers involved may be large does not appear to me to make any difference to the principle to be applied ... And this, I think, must be the case whether the relationship be near or distant, whether it is limited to one generation or is extended to two or three or in perpetuity."*

Education and Charity:

The next question or element for Lord Greene to consider was whether gifts for the advancement of education may be included under "charitable trusts". Lord Greene cited a legal literature, Tudor on Charities which answered this question in affirmative, and cited three cases which *Tudor on Charities* [7] relied on for its argument. Lord Greene then analysed the judgments of the cases in turn, and for the purpose of simplicity is here omitted, to which he concluded that the arguments in cases which supported the inclusion of educational gift under charitable trusts, are, in his opinion, incorrect. Lord Greene argued that much of the decisions were ambiguous in why educational gifts are charitable trusts, where he stated, *"I do not regard this as a satisfactory decision. There was no argument; the learned judge without giving any reasons treated the gift as one*

---

[7] HG Carter & FM Crawshaw, *Tudor on Charities* (5th edn, Sweet & Maxwell 1929).

教育和慈善：

格林大法官需要考虑的下一个问题或要素是，用于促进教育的赠物是否可以包括在“慈善信托”中。格林大法官引用了一部法律文献《都铎论慈善》[7]（对该问题持肯定回答）和该书为其观点所依赖的3个案例。随后，格林大法官依次分析了这些案件的判决。为了简单起见，此处省略。格林大法官得出结论，在他看来，支持将教育捐赠纳入慈善信托的案件中的论点并不正确。格林大法官论及，其中很多判决在谈及为什么教育捐赠是慈善信托方面均模棱两可，他说：“我不认为这是一个令人满意的决定。其没有任何论点；博学的法官在没有给出任何理由的情况下，将该捐赠视为有利于一部分公众的捐赠。”

[7] 哈里·格雷厄姆、弗兰克·麦肯齐：《都铎论慈善》（第5版），斯威特与马克斯韦尔出版公司1929年版。

in favour of a section of the public."

To counter Tudor on Charities and the cases which it relied on, Lord Greene cited a case which achieved certain levels of clarity on the tension between educational gifts and charitable trusts, where Barton J in an Irish case, *Laverty v Laverty* said, *"In my opinion, a valid charitable trust might be created for the advancement of education, with a preference for persons of a particular surname, either by the endowment of or gift to a school or college."* [8] One can infer from Barton J's judgment that the gift may not be addressed directly to the trustee as an individual for the benefit of specific individuals, but instead directed towards an institution, such as a school or college where the overall motive is a charitable one. Ultimately Lord Greene in the present case stated, *"I am of opinion that a gift for the education of descendants of named persons must be regarded as a family trust and not as one for the benefit of a section of the community."*

The "poor relations" cases:

The primary reason that the first instance judge, Cohen J. held that the trust in question were a valid one was due to his inability to disregard the "poor relations" cases. The poor relations cases are a group of past authoritative cases which stated that gifts to the poor relations of the testator should be considered charitable. The gifts in this case are left for the benefit of the descendants of three families,

[8] Laverty v Laverty, [1907] 1 I. R. 9.

为了与《都铎论慈善》及其所依赖的案例抗衡，格林大法官引用了一个案例，该案例在一定程度上明确了教育捐赠与慈善信托之间的紧张关系，巴顿法官在一个爱尔兰案例——拉维蒂诉拉维蒂案中说，“**我认为，可以通过向学校或学院以捐赠或赠物的方式，设立一个有效的慈善信托，以促进教育并优先考虑某一姓氏的人**”。[8] 从巴顿法官的判决可以推断，赠物不能直接给予作为个人的受托人，以使特定的个人受益，而是指向一个机构，如学校或学院，其总体动机是慈善。最终，格林大法官在本案中指出：“**我认为，为指名人士的后裔提供教育的赠物必须视为家庭信托，而不是为社区某一部分人的利益而提供。**”

“贫困亲属”案例：

一审法官科恩认为，所涉信托是有效信托的主要原因是他无法无视“贫困亲属”案件。贫困亲属案是一组过去的权威性案例，认定赠与给立遗嘱人的贫困亲属的赠物应被视为慈善。该案件中的赠物是留给 3 个家庭的后代，我们在此无法获得关于这些后代或他们各自的家庭是否富有的信息，但是由于科恩法官依赖于贫困亲属的论点，我们可以推断他们可能被推测处

[8] 拉维蒂诉拉维蒂案，[1907] 1 I. R. 9。

and we are here unable to obtain the information on how wealthy or not these descendants or their respective families are, though since Cohen J relied on the poor relations argument one may infer that they might be on the poorer side of the speculations.

I will address only one of the countless cases mentioned, *Issac v De Friez*, as all subsequent cases relied on the decision of this case. In Issac, the gifts were, *"(1) a gift of two annuities to the poorest relations of the testator and of his wife; (2) a gift of income to one poor relation of the testator 'for a portion in the way of marriage and putting him or her out in the world,' and (3) a similar gift of income to one poor relation of his wife."* [9] Those gifts were held to be valid charitable gifts, but the judge failed to explain sufficiently his reasons of doing so. Lord Greene in the present case believed that all the cases which followed the ruling in Issac failed to question the correctness of the decision, and that he was of opinion to overrule the rules laid out in Issac and all the "poor relations" cases. However, Lord Greene stated that since the poor relations cases had been followed by countless families for generations, it would be impossible to completely overrule this doctrine, but he merely stated that the Court of Appeal in this case does not have to be bound by this decision.

Ultimately, Lord Greene and the rest of the judges in the Court of Appeal allowed the appeal and reversed the decision made by the first instance judge. The trust in question was held to be an invalid

---

[9] Issac v De Friez 2 Amb. 595.

于比较贫困的一方。

笔者将仅讨论所提到的不可胜数的案件中的一个，即伊萨克诉德弗里斯案，因随后的所有案件均依赖于该案的判决。在伊萨克案中，赠物是，“(1)向立遗嘱人及其妻子最贫穷的亲属赠送两年的资金；(2)将收入赠与立遗人的一个贫苦亲属，以‘资助婚姻的一部分，并使他或她在世界上生活’，以及(3)给他妻子的一个贫困亲属类似的收入赠物”。[9] 这些赠物被认为是有效的慈善赠物，但法官没有充分解释他这样认定的理由。格林大法官在本案中认为，在伊萨克案判决之后的所有案件均没有质疑该判决的正确性，他认为可以推翻伊萨克案和所有“贫困亲属”案件中确定的规则。然而，格林大法官指出，由于贫困亲属案件已经被无数家庭世代遵循，不可能去完全推翻这一理论，但格林大法官指出，本案上诉法院不必受这一判决的约束。

最终，格林大法官和上诉法院的其他法官支持了上诉并推翻了一审判决。所涉信托被认定为无效的慈善信托，因为“受益人是根据个人关系界定的，缺乏作为公众信托的性质”。

[9] 伊萨克诉德弗里斯案，2 Amb. 595。

charitable trust, as *"the beneficiaries were defined by reference to a personal relationship, and it lacked the quality of being a public trust."*

Comments

The charitable trusts' power to evade the perpetuity rule had been incorrectly utilized by many UK or Irish nationals in establishing charitable trusts for the "public", while only benefiting those they care for. The Court of Appeal in this case demonstrated an exceptional thought process and courage to hold these similar trusts void and clarify the definition of "public". However, specifically one part of the judgments provided certain levels of uncertainty, as Lord Greene's decision to disregard the "poor relations" cases but not completely overrule them casts shadows on how future charity trusts cases should be dealt with. We may infer that this present case renders the "poor relations" cases voidable, but not completely void, thereby it is for the judges to hold discretion over this matter.

案件评述

许多英国或爱尔兰国民在为“公众”设立慈善信托时，错误地利用了慈善信托规避永久性规则的权力，而只惠及他们所关心的人。上诉法院在本案中展示了一种特殊的思维过程和勇气，其认为这些类似的信托无效，并澄清了“公众”的定义。然而，判决的某一部分提供了一定程度的不确定性，因为格林大法官决定无视“贫困亲属”案件，但没有完全推翻它们，这给未来的慈善信托案件应该如何处理埋下了阴影。我们可以推断，本案使“贫困亲属”案件可以无效，但并非完全无效，因此法官在该类案件上拥有自由裁量权。